HOW TO TRADE STOCKS CHEAP

The Essential Guide to Reducing Your Stock Trading Costs, Protecting Gains, and Managing Risk

by Chad Austin

Disclaimer: I wrote this book myself and it reflects my own opinions. I do not own or recommend any of the stocks referenced in this book. Any calculations and trading examples are intended to be accurate and illustrative, but cannot be guaranteed as such. Trading stocks is an inherently risky activity and can result in sudden and significant losses. It is not suitable for everyone. I present myself as an author and not a stockbroker, broker-dealer, financial advisor, investment advisor, accountant, or in the business of giving financial advice. This book is written for general information purposes only. I share ideas and make recommendations that should not be taken as personal investment advice. This book is not intended to replace the guidance and expertise of a licensed financial professional. I am not responsible for the inaccuracy or misuse of the information provided. Use of the strategies and information contained in this book is at the sole choice and risk of the reader.

www.TradeStocksCheap.com

ISBN-10: 1534621148
ISBN-13: 978-1534621145

TABLE OF CONTENTS

Why I Wrote This Book

I am not a financial professional. I am a quality manager by trade with over 20 years' experience inspecting, testing, documenting, and reporting issues found in complex software and hardware systems. This gives me a unique perspective on finding out how things work and revealing weaknesses in things that many people fail to recognize. I recommend solutions for solving these problems, cutting waste, reducing risk, saving time, and lowering costs for all involved.

Investing in the stock market for nearly two decades, I made a lot of money and lost a lot of money. I read myriad stock and finance books, followed trends, reviewed financial reports, and made countless trades. Once I began to analyze my trading expenses with my accountant, we found I was wasting money each year, sometimes on bad stock picks (no one is perfect), but more often on commissions, fees, and taxes related to trading.

After I finally calculated what my true costs of trading were, I was in shock. I was bleeding cash and I didn't even know it. I am a smart guy, how did this happen? The quest was on to figure out the best ways to trade stocks for less.

Because I had learned so much about reducing trading costs as well as trading risks and then implementing those strategies successfully, I felt qualified and excited to share this information with others. This book is a culmination of years of trial and error, countless trading hours, diligent research, and continuous education. I want you to benefit from my mistakes and learn what I discovered.

About This Book

This book is for trading stocks in long positions in the United States, though many of the strategies are internationally applicable. The book does not cover shorting stocks, stock speculating, day trading, options, commodities, currencies, mutual funds, etc., as those areas are quite different specialties and have their own strategies and methods worthy of their own books. As stated in the disclaimer, trading stocks is inherently risky. The risk can never be eliminated and despite being easy to get started, stock trading may not be suitable for everyone.

This book is designed to provide clear and useful money-saving concepts to you, the solo trader, eager to make and retain trading capital. You will learn about important trading terms, types of brokerages, buying and selling stocks, protecting gains, and risk management methods.

In this book, I make the assumption that you know at least the basics of stock trading but do my best to explain my ideas in simple terms so even a novice can comprehend what I am trying to convey. There are many great books on the mechanics and analysis of the stock market and how to choose stocks. I suggest you read as much as you can and never stop learning. This book is just one rung on your ladder to success.

The book is geared towards the individual trader who wants to better understand stock trading costs and how to control them. Even if you are more advanced in your trading knowledge, this book is a good refresher on some key principles and contains some useful ideas perhaps you have not considered before. I certainly hope so.

Attention Hawk-Eyed Readers: This book was reviewed and proofread by editing professionals before it was released to you but if by chance you find a misspelling or other simple error that we missed please report it to us. If you are the first to let us know, you'll get a special gift as a gesture of appreciation.

Send To: corrections@tradestockscheap.com

Introduction

Congratulations on taking the first step toward getting your stock trading costs under control. Whether you are new to trading or have been at it for a while, this book is designed to give you practical, real-world methods to preserve your investment capital for what really matters, purchasing stocks.

If you don't know what type of trader you are or would like to become, I provide some ideas on how to figure this out. But only you can answer that question honestly. Never take on more risk than you are able to manage. If you would worry all night about holding a stock for fear of loss or don't have enough money to trade without sacrificing food, there are safer ways to utilize your capital.

Even if you are not in the market at all, don't worry. Getting started is not difficult. This book covers the basics of getting a new brokerage account set up correctly, which can give you a leg up on people who fail to take the time to research.

The stock market is a tremendous money making opportunity that many people think they simply can't figure out or don't have access to. Times have been tough in recent years and you may think you just don't have the resources to be in the stock market, but as you will soon see, the market is available to you and easy to access and with only a small amount of money to start trading. I have done it and I know you can too!

I hope this book helps take some of the mystery and fear out of stock trading and gives you the information and encouragement to trade stocks cheap.

Chapter 1. Getting Started

Trading Vs. Investing

I have been asked, what is the difference between trading and investing in stocks? It's a great question and worthy of clarification.

An investor will plan to buy a stock with the intent of holding it for a longer time frame planning on the equity appreciating during that period. An investor may buy a stock and hold it for a year and often longer. Obviously, he may sell it sooner if there is a significant gain or the company has a fundamental problem that will not be resolved but the goal is to buy and hold.

A trader typically refers to a person who buys stocks not necessarily for the long term. He will take profits when he can or sell to limit losses if the stock goes in the wrong direction. A trader may buy a stock today and sell today or buy today and sell in two months. A trader is not necessarily a day trader as many people assume. Day traders typically won't hold any stock more than a day, hence the name.

I use the term trading stocks in this book to refer to an individual who buys and sells a stock. Regardless of whether you are an investor or trader, this book is designed to cover methods to save and protect your hard earned money. Both traders and investors have to buy and sell their stock and both will benefit by controlling the costs associated with those trades.

Your Goals

Modern technology makes it very easy to open a brokerage account for a very small amount of funding capital and start trading quickly, but that is just the beginning of your journey to success. Your goals may be simply to make a few extra dollars to supplement your income or you may want to commit to a life of trading as your full-time career. The choice is yours and I encourage you to take this section seriously and know why you want to trade.

I was so excited when I started and I had no idea what I was doing. My goal was to pick a hot biotech stock and retire early. Well, needless to say, that did not happen, but I sure learned a lot as a result of poor planning and weak discipline.

If you are the type of trader who has ample trading funds, but little time to research, execute your own trades, and don't mind paying a broker to assist you, you will be less interested in saving money on fees and more interested in the assistance of a full-service brokerage. However, if you are like many millions of people who are looking to trade on your own and you need to be thrifty, this book offers helpful information to aid you in your quest.

Stock Markets

What types of stocks are you interested in trading? If you don't know, you should think about it. If you are going to simply trade the big stocks on the major exchanges like the New York Stock Exchange (NYSE) and National Association of Securities Dealers Automated Quotations (Nasdaq) then you will be less picky than if you are going to trade Over-The-Counter (OTC) stocks or on foreign exchanges. Some brokerages charge additional fees to trade OTC or foreign stocks. Even worse, they may not allow you to trade them at all thus limiting your options.

Here is an overview of basic stock categories and how they might affect your trading expenses and risks:

Major U.S. Stocks

If you are based in the United States, the easiest stocks to trade will be the ones listed on the larger exchanges such as NYSE or Nasdaq. There are thousands of great companies listed in these markets and trading them is easy and straightforward. Any type of brokerage from full-service to discount will let you trade them. The liquidity makes the process less risky giving you the overall best chances of keeping your trading costs low.

Key Points:

- Lower Risk
- Good Liquidity
- Easy to Trade
- Well-Known Companies

Foreign Stocks

Many investors are looking for greater diversity in their portfolio. A common recommendation is to expand their investments into the foreign markets such as the Asian or European exchanges. This can indeed keep some of your money shielded from total exposure to a U.S. based portfolio, but it can also bring more risk than it is worth for the retail investor.

I think of it as speaking a foreign language. I know enough Spanish to be dangerous so I don't usually speak it. I don't know enough about foreign exchanges and companies to trade them comfortably so I prefer not to participate. If you intend to trade in foreign stocks, be aware of the challenges and unique issues you may encounter and do the necessary due diligence to be competent.

The Securities and Exchange Commission (SEC) offers a good explanation of the foreign investing practice and associated risks if you are considering this type of trading.

SEC International Investing Guide
http://www.sec.gov/investor/pubs/ininvest.htm

Key Points:

- Diversification Benefits
- Liquidity Issues
- Transparency Issues
- Currency Exchange Issues
- Additional Trading Fees
- Brokerage Restrictions

Micro-Cap Stocks

Micro-cap stocks are advertised all over the place now. I even heard radio spots touting the latest millionaire-making opportunity. The SEC classifies micro-cap companies as having a low market capitalization (under $250 million) compared to other companies listed on the major exchanges.

One popular group of micro-cap stocks is OTC

(over-the-counter) companies. They are a micro-cap subset categorized as Nano-Cap (less than $50 million market cap). Due to the very low capitalization, accompanying volatility, and inherent risk associated with them, these stocks are usually not traded on the major exchanges. They typically use other networks like the OTC Bulletin Board (OTCBB) to list their stock for sale. Sometimes referred to as "Penny Stock", these much riskier companies may still be regulated by the SEC to some extent. Some great companies do come from OTC and move to the major markets once they meet the more stringent requirements.

I have traded OTC stocks with mixed results so I can definitely attest to the unpredictable nature of their performance. The lure of quick riches attracts many new investors to this niche. If you intend to trade any OTC stocks it is imperative that you learn everything you can about the pitfalls and unique rules associated with them. There can often be significant fees and limitations to trading OTC with many brokerages so know that before you start.

The SEC provides a good explanation and guidance on investing in micro-cap stocks.

SEC Micro-Cap Stock Guide
https://www.sec.gov/investor/pubs/microcapstock.htm

Key Points:

- Small Companies
- Liquidity Issues
- Transparency Issues
- Brokerage Fees
- Brokerage Restrictions

Further Thoughts

Still not sure where to start? You are not alone. I went through this when I got started. If you think you might need professional help, a registered investment adviser could be a great resource even if you intend to trade stocks on your own. An adviser will work with you and your goals to help manage the process and provide critical guidance on how to invest, manage, and grow the money you earn trading stocks on your own, so the two go hand in hand. I cover more on getting professional help in Chapter 7.

What if you don't have or want an investment adviser? This is where you need to ask yourself some serious questions to help you create a plan, in addition to educating yourself continually on everything about stocks and investing.

Risk Assessment

Your assignment is to perform a basic risk self-assessment using the following questions and answer them honestly. This exercise will give you a good idea of how conservative you should trade. Obviously, the less risk tolerant you are, the less money you have, and the less knowledge you have about stocks your trading should be very conservative. I tend to believe in taking a low risk and cautious approach to trading especially if you are just starting out.

Some good risk assessment questions are:

- How much do you know about trading stock?
- How much time do you have to research and educate yourself?
- Are you looking to invest long-term or trade stocks to generate income today?
- How much money do you have to trade with?
- What types of stocks do you intend to trade?
- What is your risk tolerance?

Chapter 2. Stock Trading Costs

This might seem obvious to some, but it's good to start by understanding exactly what kinds of fees and expenses are likely to be associated with the trading of stocks.

Even though this book focuses on reducing or eliminating your trading costs, it's important to remember brokerages offer access to a highly complex and costly trading platform that takes money to run. I never feel bad about paying for the ability to buy and sell stocks when necessary. It is, after all, a free market so a good service is worth paying for, but don't pay too much.

Trading Equipment

When you go fishing, do you just jump in your car and head to the lake without getting your fishing gear? A fishing rod, reel, tackle, and bait are the very basics you need to catch a fish. Trading stocks is no different in terms of minimal tools to conduct business. The tools are not expensive and you probably already have them, but I would be remiss if I didn't cover the basic equipment for a stock trader.

Home Trading

I like to trade from the comfort of my home desk. I can control the environment, put on some relaxing music, sit in my favorite chair, and use my personal computer, which I have configured for an optimal trading experience. You may be able to duplicate this at your office if you have a regular job, but many employers frown upon trading at work so always be aware of the rules if you want to use your employer's resources.

Desktop Computer

If you use a desktop computer, you will need a mouse, keyboard, monitor, and Internet access. The mouse and keyboard don't have to be special, but it is nice to have a keyboard with a 10 key number pad. I use this often to crunch numbers as I plan my trades. If you don't have one, get a cheap calculator. The monitor is more important to help you trade and you should buy as big a monitor as you can afford. If you look at professional traders' desktops, they usually have multiple monitors all displaying various market data. I have one large monitor with multiple windows up simultaneously, but you can experiment with what works best for you. A good 23" flat panel monitor can cost under $200 and that is a good size to allow multiple window displays.

Internet access is also a very important consideration, but not so much speed as reliability. Having your Internet disconnect during a trade is dangerous.

It would also be helpful to have a phone at your trading desk. This can be a mobile or land line, just so long as you have good reception. If something happens and you need to call your broker, it's one more layer of technology to help you if something fails. Things do fail, especially when you don't want them to.

Internet brokerages have high-level security built into their websites so be sure you have and are able to get the latest web browser installed on your trading computer.

When you are selecting your brokerage, check to see if it has any proprietary software required for using its trading system. If it does, it may only run on a Windows computer so if you use an Apple computer you may have issues.

Trader Tip: It's ok if you don't have the latest computer or fancy monitor. You can probably trade stocks with the equipment you have. I have a 10-year-old desktop that I was able to update to allow me to trade. If your computer or operating system is old and you aren't sure if it will work, brokerages will publish their minimum system requirements on their website support section so make sure to check before you open an account.

Mobile Trading

Trading from the road is often an option provided you have prepared in advance. Whether you prefer a laptop or mobile device, it's wise to have your equipment up to date and ready to go when the need to make a trade arises.

Laptop Computer

Modern laptops are powerful, easy to use, and much cheaper than they used to be. You can get a decent laptop these days for under $300 so this is a good option if you are going to be away from home frequently. The keyboard, mouse, and monitor are built in so all you will need is a good Internet service.

Smartphone or Tablet

Even a roaming rock climber can trade stocks. You don't need to be indoors when you trade, but make sure you have a reliable and easy to use smartphone or tablet and a good cellular carrier or Wi-Fi for the areas you spend the most time.

When selecting a brokerage, check that it has an app or a mobile optimized website that works with your device and operating system. Always keep the device and your trading software updated to make sure you have everything you need when it's time to make a trade. Another cheap mobile tool is a backup battery charger. You can get one at a convenience store for $5. If you're trying to make an important trade with a dying battery, it could save the day.

Commissions

Commissions on orders are the primary revenue generator for your brokerage on the retail investor side. This will commonly be the trading cost you can control by selecting the right brokerage, controlling your trading frequency, and performing the work of placing orders yourself.

Order Entry Types

There are three primary order entry types for trading stocks: Placing orders online (self-entered orders via your brokerage website), broker-assisted orders (broker entered orders via a registered stockbroker), and telephone orders (Interactive Voice Response, or IVR, orders placed by you by phone.). Each of these types has specific prices and procedures.

Broker-Assisted Order

Stockbrokers will gladly place an order for you by

phone or in person and at times, there may be a need to get their help. Sometimes you may be trying to enter an order for more shares than your access allows, for example. Another scenario is when you have a stock that had special restrictions applied to it that would require a stockbroker to help you place the order. I have had many good experiences using a stockbroker to help me with a trade, but as with getting help from any professional, it costs more money.

The fees for a broker-assisted trade vary between brokerages, but you can expect to pay a minimum of $30 per transaction. If you use a broker to place your orders to buy and to sell a position, the commissions would be $60 total. As mentioned in the examples above, you may need help with a trade. The math works if your projected gains are sufficient to offset the added cost. In general, I don't call a broker unless there is a pressing need.

Phone Order

I am sure you have called a bank, utility, or retailer for help and had to deal with a fancy automated phone tree following the prompts and speaking or pressing numbers. Hurray! You have already used an IVR system, (Interactive Voice Response). Like any large business, your brokerage will likely have this system in place to manage your call if you need to contact them.

In addition to helping you with your account balance

or change your password, you can place a trade using IVR, as well. Similar to a broker-assisted order, IVR will cost you more money to enter an order. The IVR fee is similar to the broker-assisted fee at around $30 per order, but can be higher or lower depending on the brokerage. You can usually plan to not use this option often, but you may find yourself in a remote location with no Internet access and adequate cell coverage. In that instance using an IVR order makes sense if you need to enter an order in a pinch.

Online Order

Conducting a stock trade from your computer, smartphone, or tablet using your brokerage's website or app is considered an online trade. The access to the Electronic Communication Network (ECN) is authorized through your account and you can enter the orders yourself. Because your brokerage doesn't need to assign a person to handle the transaction you get a discount on the order commission. As you might guess, this will be your best option to reduce fees when you trade.

Online orders often cost far less than broker-assisted or IVR orders with a wide range of prices from brokerage to brokerage. On average, anything less than $10 per trade is a decent price to pay. Knowing trade commissions will be one of your biggest trading expenses you will incur, spend the time to find the brokerage that works best for you and has the lowest online trade commissions. The brokerages I use the most have online trade fees much less than $10, so shop around.

Hidden Fees

On average, less than one percent of people take the time to read the fine print online. It's no surprise that many pay for this oversight. Before selecting a brokerage or using a financial service, be aware that there are sometimes hidden fees. They really aren't so much hidden as "strategically located". You just need to know where to look.

One source of hidden fees is brokerage account fees. You will want to go to the fee schedule first, by law, they will have to disclose what they will be charging for. Some examples could be account maintenance fees, minimum balance fees, transfer fees, sales charges, inactivity fees, etc. Be sure to thoroughly research any brokerage you are thinking about using regardless of its reputability to make sure there are no costs that are not initially obvious to you.

Example: Say your brokerage has a minimum account balance of $2,500 and you have a financial emergency so you take out some of your money lowering your balance below the minimum. What you may not have known is the brokerage charges you $50 for dropping below the minimum amount. You just paid $50 you could have avoided had you chose a brokerage that didn't have the minimum balance requirement penalty. Read the fine print!

Trading Information

It goes without saying that trading stocks is a rapidly changing information dependent activity. There are so many sources for tools, community, analysis, and news for traders. To top it off, many of the sites that advertise the best, fastest, or most trusted information charge you for it and it may not be worth it. There are some very good sources of all the trading information you could ever read that are free.

To help you get started with some good free sources of news, analysis, tools, community, education, and stock information, I picked some of the providers I use and find most helpful and generally have good user ratings. By no means is this a complete list. In fact, you may find better sources that I have not covered here. I encourage you to always be searching for the best trading tools for you and not feel limited by what others tell you to use.

News, Research, Community, Quoting

In my early days, I signed up for a lot of stock information services, some free and some fee-based. Often they claimed to give the investor winning trades or keys to stock market riches. The reality is I spent a lot of money and time getting questionable research and information that I could have gotten for free had I investigated all the options that were out there. One year I paid $300 on analyst reports, $100 on premium message boards, $600 on Level II stock quotes, $300 on research tools, in addition to $1,000 plus in trading fees. What was I thinking? I get all that information for FREE now and I'll show you how.

My friends who don't trade say, "That seems like an awful lot of stuff just to buy some stock!" I say trading stocks is like captaining a ship. You have multiple screens and gauges in front of you displaying all the critical data you need to guide your way and help you avoid the rocks.

I like to have a few key stock sites up when I trade giving me a breadth of intelligence prior to making a trading decision. After all, not every site will have all the information all the time, and more is better when it comes to knowledge. In addition to their trading platform, the professional traders I have watched have several of the sites I mention in this book up at the same time in different browser windows, monitoring the data constantly.

Stock News

Financial news sources are everywhere now. Not all of them are free and not all of them are good. I have put together a list of a few that I use often and are free and reliable:

Benzinga

Benzinga is quickly becoming a cornerstone in the financial news and stock market information business. Benzinga describes themselves as a full-service news and media company specializing in real-time news, actionable trading ideas, and insightful commentary. After using their service for a while now, I can say that they live up to their claims.

Benzinga offers not just news, but also provides very useful market updates, corporate ratings, trade ideas, and helpful personal finance feeds. Much of the information is available anonymously, but if you want more advanced features such as watch lists and alerts you, will need to create a free account. Benzinga does provide a great mobile app now so you can access your customized account information on the go.

Benzinga
Site: http://www.benzinga.com
Content: Financial News, Stock Information, Quotes, Charts, Watch Lists, Mobile App
Price: Free

CNBC

CNBC has been around for years and is one of the most-used and trusted financial news networks. In addition to its great financial television programs, CNBC's website is also an excellent resource for traders. Their easy to use and convenient mobile app provides the functionality of the website in a streamlined mobile format. It is a must-have if you are a mobile user.

One outstanding feature of the app is the news and portfolio alerts that let you know when events pertaining to your stocks occur. You just need to create an account, which is quick and easy. Not only can you track and manage your stocks and view real-time market summaries, you will be able to get access to clips of most of the CNBC shows in the video section, which I like to watch if I am away from my television during the trading day. If you happen to have a cable or satellite television package, you can use the app to watch CNBC TV live. How cool is that?

CNBC
Site: http://www.cnbc.com
Content: Financial News, Stock Information, Quotes, Charts, Watch Lists, Alerts, Financial Video Feeds, Mobile App
Price: Free

Google Finance

Google has become a household name for searching the web, but did you know it has an excellent stock news and finance section? Constantly adding features and functionality, Google Finance offers great stock and financial news for U.S. and global markets, stock screeners, current stock trends, stock quotes, and portfolio manager. The portfolio manager allows you to enter all your cash holdings and stock positions with buy price, share quantity, and trade commissions. Google will keep track of your portfolio's performance over time. A key benefit to anyone who already has a Gmail or Google account is that all this can be saved using your existing login.

Google Finance
Site: https://www.google.com/finance
Content: Financial News, Stock Information, Quotes, Charts, Portfolio Manager, Watch Lists, Alerts, Google Account Integration
Price: Free

Research and Analysis

Stock analysis can be broken down into two general categories, third-party analysis performed by industry professionals and analysis you personally perform.

Professional Analysis

The first type of investment analysis is usually a paid service or individual report that is provided by an independent third-party firm that analyzes a stock. Some popular names of analysis firms are Zacks, Morningstar, and Argus Research. These types of analysis can most commonly be found free as part of your brokerage service but individual reports and subscriptions can usually be purchased independently.

Personal Analysis

The second type of analysis is the kind you do yourself. As I mentioned earlier in this book, stock analysis is a key part of your due diligence in evaluating any stock you are interested in. The following are several great analysis oriented websites that are very popular among traders and have great free resources:

Barchart

Barchart is a very helpful site providing analysis and charting tools. I keep the site open during my trading day and really like the simple and easy-to-navigate layout. Barchart offers a wide array of services including powerful market screeners, downloadable historical data, charting, portfolio tracking, price alerts, personalized market feeds, investor education, video headlines, and trader community. It does have some paid services, but most general information is available at no cost. For a more customized experience, create a free account and personalize the information the way you want it.

One very popular and really helpful feature is the Barchart Opinion page. Select a stock you are interested in analyzing, select Barchart Opinion and you get a market snapshot of common short-, medium-, and long-term indicators so you can see the buy and sell signals at a glance. This doesn't replace doing your own analysis, but checking Barchart Opinion first will give you a good idea of what direction the stock is likely to move.

The community component includes interactive user voting for stocks and exchanges. The site also has several great daily newsletters, the Barchart "Morning Call" and the Barchart "Chart of the Day." The Morning Call gives you great insight into the coming day's trading and things to watch for. The Chart of the Day gives an excellent analysis of a featured stock each day that gives a basic synopsis of fundamental and technical analysis in quick and easy to understand format.

More recently, Barchart has created a mobile app that gives you all the content via a convenient mobile platform. You can track your watch lists, view market news, and charts as well as screeners for the day's stock action by volume, momentum, highs, lows, and much more.

Barchart
Site: https://www.barchart.com
Content: Financial News, Stock Information,
Quotes, Charts, Portfolio Manager, Analysis Tools,
Market Information, Mobile App
Price: Free

Seeking Alpha

A very popular and information-packed stock trading portal, Seeking Alpha offers traders of all levels something useful. Its audience is diverse and includes 4 million registered users, including 18 percent of financial professionals. In addition to its breadth of fundamental research and analysis, Seeking Alpha has over 10,000 contributing authors, which covered over 4,000 small and midcap stocks in one year.

Some useful content it provides is custom portfolios, unique and informative articles, as well as insightful easy to understand opinion and analysis of thousands of stocks. All this is provided free to traders, but they do offer a professional package with unique in-depth research summaries if you find you want more. Seeking Alpha also offers access to your customized account experience in a high-ranking convenient mobile app.

Seeking Alpha
Site: https://www.seekingalpha.com
Content: Financial News, Stock Information, Quotes, Charts, Portfolio Manager, Alerts, Analysis Tools, Analyst Opinions, Mobile App
Price: Free

Finviz

Short for Financial Visualizations, Finviz is a high-tech online cockpit of all the stock data you would need to perform your own exhaustive analysis. Given the wealth of information available at Finviz, the site is remarkably clean and well organized.

The stock screener is a very powerful filtering tool allowing you to select a specific exchange, market cap, target price, index, sector, analysis recommendation, volume, industry, and many other variables. Once you have the data sorted, you can select a stock that meets your criteria and get a detailed chart along with relevant stock data, analyst opinions, and news. When you find a stock you want to track, save your choice to your portfolio. Also integrated into social media, Finviz allows you to customize and publish charts to share with your friends via Twitter and Facebook.

All this is provided for free. Custom portfolio management will require a simple account be created. Advanced features such as real-time quotes, intraday charts, screener presets, customized layouts, and data export are available as part of the premium FINVIZ*Elite service if you find their product worth the money.

Finviz
Site: http://www.finviz.com
Content: Stock Charts, Heat Maps, Screeners,
Portfolio Manager, Analysis Tools, Opinions
Price: Free

Stock Communities

I am sure you know how powerful social media is in our lives today. From sharing family photos to collaborating at work, social media helps us connect to friends, family, and colleagues around the globe. How relevant is this to trading stocks? The social element is very relevant.

I originally started my trading life as a solo trader doing all my own research, testing my ideas, and making trades in a social vacuum. I didn't have friends or family into the stock market so I didn't have much of an investor social network. As I matured and grew as an investor, I came to realize that stock trading is a group effort. You have brokers, buyers, sellers, and a referee called the Securities and Exchange Commission (SEC) all interacting in a large sea of information, news, regulations, and global events.

I don't trade at all now unless I get a feel for what the social signals are in the markets and stocks I am following. In the intelligence community, it is called "HUMINT", or Human Intelligence. In the stock world, it is a powerful tool to assist your trading decisions. You can only know so much about a stock at a given time, but imagine having thousands of fellow investors all sharing ideas and information on the stocks you are interested in. I often find news about stocks from social media before it hits the mainstream news outlets. I think some people never sleep.

Stocks sometimes trade on sentiment alone, independent of what the reality may actually be. It boils down to what people are thinking. It is essentially a popularity index. If you have a lot of traders excited about a stock, there are more people to push the price up. If people are very negative about a stock, the selling pressure will be higher so the price will likely start a downward movement. The human element makes this science difficult to predict, but it's just one more tool you can use during your continued due diligence.

Many stock information sites will have some sort of free community component, but if there aren't a lot of users it won't be very helpful to your trading efforts. The primary type of online community is the message board, usually referred to as simply "boards." This is where you will usually find the bulk of your social sentiment about stocks.

After years of experimenting with the various social platforms that have the most features and active users, I have put together a list of some of my favorite sites:

Board Central

Let me ask you a question. Do you have time to keep up with all the social media sources every day for every stock? I bet you said no. I don't have that kind of time either, but with this goldmine, you can track social media trends for all your stocks from multiple sources all in one spot. If social media is the kingdom, Board Central is the king of stock communities.

Board Central is an award-winning social media aggregator site for stock information and allows you to quickly see the latest news and community postings from Yahoo, Investors Hub, Motley Fool, Google, Twitter, The Lion, Investor Village, and more. All you have to do is enter a ticker symbol and select the type of information you want to see from message boards, tweets, or social profiles. Key highlighted features of Board Central are Web BuZZ, StockTalk, and Most Popular, each giving a different social perspective on stocks and markets. If you had to choose just one site for your social perspective on stocks, this would be it.

Board Central
Site: http://www.boardcentral.com
Content: Stock Message Boards,
Social Media Aggregator
Price: Free

Investors Hub

Investors Hub, sometimes referred to as iHub, is a social treasure trove for all things stocks. I will preface my review by saying Investors Hub has been controversial at times. As with any popular platform, it has some lovers and some haters. There are always promoters and bashers of stocks out there. Always take what any one person or "expert" says with a grain of salt. It's the general community feeling for a stock you want from any social media site. A good strategy is always to research stock information yourself and verify anything you hear. The Internet in some ways is the modern Wild West and you never know the motives of people in social media.

Boasting over 550,000 members, 120,000,000 messages on more than 25,000 message boards, the amount of social sentiment you can find on iHub is staggering. It covers a wide variety of stocks and exchanges, including penny and foreign stocks.

One of the key features that I find useful, The Ticker Buzz Cloud, scans all the boards for the greatest percentage of posts in the past 24 hours gives you a quick view of what is hot at any given moment. The most active boards are helpful in determining what people are talking and reading about and loosely correspond to market interest in a given stock. I tend to stay away from any stock that has little or no board activity as it often translates into low stock interest and trading volume.

Its mobile application is pretty sophisticated. Create multiple monitors that track all the stocks you are following and click on each individual stock to see a quick chart and basic quote, trade volume, news, and the message board for that stock.

The service is free, but the stock quotes are delayed 15 minutes in the free account. I don't use this for my real-time, but it does have a paid service I used for years if you want to upgrade. Registration is simple and allows you to interact with the community, bookmark your favorite message boards, and post your own messages to join the conversation.

Investors Hub
Site: http://www.investorshub.advfn.com
Content: Stock Message Boards, News, Watch Lists, Charts, Mobile App
Price: Free

StockTwits®

The world's largest social network catering to traders, StockTwits® is one of the top five stock sites I use on a regular basis. Hundreds of thousands of investors, market pros, and companies are online sharing trades, ideas, and information on stocks for most of the popular exchanges. It's a fun and engaging user experience that really captures the essence of a good online interactive community.

StockTwits® features trending heat maps, Yahoo and CNN Money news, Twitter, LinkedIn, and Facebook integration as well as account linking to trading apps such as Robinhood, which further enhances the service's cross platform appeal.

StockTwits®
Site: http://www.stocktwits.com
Content: Stock Community, Watch Lists, News, Charts, Mobile App
Price: Free

Price Quotes

Stock price quotes are everywhere you look these days. You see them online, in the newspapers, and even streaming on billboards on city buildings. In many cases, however, that quote is old information.

I am often surprised at how many retail traders don't know a lot about the market quoting system even though it can dramatically improve their trading game. It goes without saying that every second counts when trading stocks and with computerized high-frequency trading becoming the norm, you need to act quickly when trying to get your orders filled at the best price possible.

The worst case is that the stock quotes are a day old when you check the financial page in the paper while enjoying your morning coffee. Best case is your quotes are real-time electronic quotes from a reliable source. Even if you think you are OK with the quotes you are currently using, read the fine print. Some of the readily available electronic quotes you see all over the Internet are delayed 15 or 20 minutes. That may sound fast, but you need much better quotes if you are to get the best prices on the stocks you trade.

Quote Levels

Quoting is a service that provides the prices and sales information for a given stock at regular intervals. There are several quote types with each incremental level having its own tier of information provided, access restrictions, and cost. The more advanced the quote, the more technical, and expensive it becomes. Some levels are not even available to the average investor. Quotes can be a confusing topic so I'll start by giving a quick overview of the three primary stock quoting levels and their relevance to your stock trading:

Level I (Level 1, L1, L I, Li) – A basic quoting service that may or may not be real-time and is often provided free as a feature on many financial websites. Information included is bid and ask quotations (what traders are offering to buy and sell a stock for) and the last sale information for a given security on a given stock exchange. The quotes are usually displayed with a corresponding color red or green with red indicating a trade with a price below the last sale price and green being a trade made above the previous sale price. This is a good start to help you get better pricing on your orders, but could be delayed for many stocks and tells you very little about the market maker price action behind the scenes which is provided with a Level 2 quote.

Level II (Level 2, L2, L II, Lii) – A more advanced quoting level that is usually a pay-to-play service and is essential for any serious trader. L2 includes everything from Level I quotes, but gives you a look behind the scenes of what the current demand and supply of shares at that exact moment in the trading day. Not knowing this information keeps you in the dark about where the stock price is heading.

Key information will be displayed in a colored table format with the last trade price, current bid price, the amount of shares being bid for purchase, current ask price with the amount of shares being offered for sale, and all the market makers currently involved with that stock on both the bid and ask sides of the order book.

Level III (Level 3, L3, L III, Liii) – You will not see this referenced much in your normal trading research. It is not something a retail investor has access to and is only available to the market makers who are charged with creating liquidity in the stocks by accepting the risk of holding large amounts of shares and offering the price quotes to traders.

Now that you have an idea of what the quote levels are all about, I am sure you are thinking, Can I get Level II quotes and can I get it for free? The short answer is yes and yes!

Level II service typically costs money and I have paid $30 or more monthly for this service. Competition in the free market has driven many brokerages to offer L2 quotes in some capacity to account holders even if you are not a big-time trader.

If your brokerage does not offer a good L2 service, one non-brokerage site offers free Level II quotes that I find very useful.

Level2StockQuotes.com

If you do an Internet search for free Level II stock quotes this site will come up at the top of the list. I like this site and still use it now even though I have L2 access from my brokerages.

The site offers free Level 2 stock quotes for most AMEX, NYSE, NASDAQ, and OTCBB stocks. You can set up watch lists, view price history, interact with charts, and compare stocks all on the same page. Another great feature they added is a Bloomberg TV video feed so you can watch the financial market news while you're on the site.

Level2StockQuotes.com
Site: http://www.level2stockquotes.com
Content: Level II Stock Quotes
Price: Free

Chapter 3. Brokerage Selection

Today there are many great brokerages available with a wide range of services and fees. That's the good news. What's difficult to determine is which one will offer the best value to you based on how you intend to trade.

Trading stocks can be as simple or complex as you want to make it. You can have a stock you love and want to own it for your whole life so you buy 100 shares as an investment. Alternatively, you could decide to actively trade a speculative company based on charts, fundamentals, or momentum that requires you to watch everything closely. Regardless of how detailed you get, having an inexpensive and trusted way to buy and sell your stock is critical. To a small-time retail investor, every penny counts. In many cases, with just a small amount to invest, $20, $30, $50, or even $200 in trading commission fees for a single trade could make it nearly impossible to ever see a profit on an investment.

Do you go to purchase a car without doing your homework about the car and dealer first? If you do, you probably won't get the best deal, you might pick a lemon, and likely won't be able to recover as much on the resale price since you paid too much. I like to think of the process of buying stocks analogous to shopping for a car and putting in the research first can make all the difference.

A busy executive with a large portfolio and high net worth may find a full-service broker the best deal forgoing cheap trades for customized one-on-one financial help. Someone who has a small amount of money to trade with and more free time could benefit more from a discount broker. So, what are all the types of brokers you can choose from?

There are three basic categories of brokerages available to a retail trader: full-service, direct-access, and discount. In addition to the traditional brokerage option, there are other methods to purchase stocks such as Direct Stock Purchase Plans.

I provide a basic description of each brokerage type and a general idea of what you could be paying in commissions. I'll list some major names in each category with an overview of features, fees, and example trading scenarios to help you in your decision-making process.

Trader Tip:

Be sure to visit http://www.TradeStocksCheap.com where you can get a free *Brokerage Comparison Tool*. I used this to screen the brokerages I use now when I was in the research stage.

Full-Service Brokerage

Once rulers of the trading world, full-service brokerages offer a full suite of services and guidance to the investor at a higher price. Some popular examples of full-service brokerages are Goldman Sachs, Edward Jones, and UBS. They are huge financial firms that typically deal with larger retail investors. Think of them as more of an asset management service than a self-serve trading account. You pay more, but you get more hands on interaction. There is often a large minimum for account balances and perhaps additional transaction fees for stock trades. There may also be maintenance fees on top of all that. I personally don't use them because my goal is to trade cheaply and under my own direction.

Depending on how much money you have and how much effort you wish to put into research and conducting your own trading, a full-service broker may be an economical choice. The upside to a full-service brokerage is that you get much more research, advice, tax guidance, and retirement planning among other custom services.

As a general guide, you could expect to pay around $50 to $200 per trade for a full-service broker. You don't need me to tell you this is a lot of money to a frugal investor, but full-service clients are investing, sometimes millions of dollars, so a few hundred per trade might not be a concern and they probably don't have the time to manage all their trades personally.

Example Trade ($200 trade commission): You buy 10 shares of XYZ at $100 per share. The commission on the single trade is $200. $100 x 10 = $1,000 in XYZ + $200 commission = $1,200 cost. That is a whopping 20 percent of the value of the stock you now own paid in commission fees. Therefore, you need a 40 percent gain just to pay for your trading commissions to close the position at break even.

Direct-Access Brokerage

Direct-access brokerages may be a good choice for a day trader or active trader. The primary benefit is to allow you to trade stocks directly with exchanges called Direct-Access Trading (DAT). Using a specialized computer program, the middleman is eliminated, increasing trade speed and quoting information. Because of the trading efficiencies, direct-access brokers may offer a pay-per-share model on stock trades or per trade commissions at a steep discount. The catch is they may charge to use their trading system, which could generate costs that consume your gains if you aren't a high volume trader.

There are a number of direct-access brokerages to choose from and what they offer for services varies. A primary shortcoming of a direct-access brokerage is a possible lack of research and trading tools found in the other brokerage types. However, if you are an adept frequent trader not needing additional brokerage services, you can save a lot of money with a DAT system. Some examples of popular direct-access brokerages are Cobra Trading, SpeedTrader, and TradeStation.

Direct-access brokerages charge from say, $0.01 commissions per share to $10 per trade. Note the flexible pricing of a direct-access may offer the ability to trade stock for a penny or less per share often with a minimum number of shares per order. Therefore, for an order to buy 100 shares in XYZ, you would pay just $1 for that trade at $0.01 per share. Not bad, but unless you meet the required trading volume in a given trading period, say 5,000 shares traded per month, you could be hit with additional fees offsetting your savings. As always, read the full fee disclosure for any brokerage to make sure you understand exactly what the costs will be.

Example Trade ($0.01 trade commission per share): You buy 100 shares of XYZ at $100 per share. The commission on the single trade is $1. So, 100 x $100 = $10,000 in XYZ + $1 commission, which adds up to $10,001 total cost. If XYZ went up to $101 per share and you sold your 100 shares for $11,000, you will only be paying $2 total for the trade commissions leaving you with $998 in gains.

Discount Brokerage

As the name suggests, discount brokerages offer the ability to trade stocks at a substantially reduced rate compared to full-service. Scottrade, E-Trade, Fidelity, and TD Ameritrade are popular examples of discount brokerages. Chances are, this will be the best category for the majority of retail traders as it combines the most features and lowest trading costs.

Inexpensive doesn't necessarily mean cheap service, even though it costs less to trade with a discount brokerage, most offer excellent research, sophisticated trading tools, and mobile apps that make the cost to feature benefit very high.

A discount brokerage will have trade commissions from around $5 to say $15. This is the greatest feature to the budget-minded trader and in a lifetime of trading, a discount brokerage will dramatically reduce your trading expenses. I personally use several discount brokerages and have been very happy with the results.

Example Trade ($10 per trade commission): You buy 1,000 shares of XYZ at $10 per share and you pay $10 for the trade. So, 1,000 shares x $10 share = $10,000 in XYZ + $10 commission, which adds up to $10,010 total cost. Add the $10 commission on the sale and you need a $0.02 gain in XYZ to cover the $20 in commissions to break even. That is certainly achievable, especially compared to the full-service example.

Commission Free Brokerage

Robinhood

A new upstart called Robinhood has entered the brokerage market with a simple mobile only free trading service. Robinhood had a staggering 700,000 people on the waiting list when they launched in 2015 indicating this could be the start of a whole new generation of free trading services in the future.

The concept is a game changer and it is surprisingly easy to get started. Just visit their website, go to the signup page, enter your contact information, link a funding bank account, submit your application, and download the app. Robinhood doesn't have a traditional broker website and relies on the mobile app for trading and managing your portfolio.

I can vouch for the simplicity of the process. I went through the setup to test it out. Just like their advertising stated, it took less than four minutes. (Yes, I timed it.)

Robinhood has no funding minimum. I got started with an initial $50 deposit (you can do less or more if you want) and once your account is approved, which didn't take long at all, only a few hours in my case, you are free to trade once your funds clear from the deposit.

There are currently some limits to the stocks you can trade, primarily U.S. stocks on major exchanges, but those are the safer exchanges, especially for the beginning trader.

The trades execute very fast and the mobile app gives you detailed information on your investment and cash balances as well as relevant news and market data from multiple sources. Link your Robinhood account to StockTwits® and you'll have a powerful community component further increasing the usefulness of both.

In case you are curious like I was, just how does Robinhood make money if they provide their service for free? The founders disclosed that they make their money from interest on the uninvested money users deposit and a margin account option further generating interest income.

If you use your smartphone to do your business like I do, this will be a welcomed addition to your arsenal of mobile trading tools. The application is very clean and simple just like their signup process with a basic and streamlined presentation that is visually pleasing and easy to navigate. You can create watch lists, view a stock chart, get basic news, check account balances, transfer money, set price alerts, and of course, buy and sell stocks.

Example Trade ($0.00 trade commission): You buy

10 shares of XYZ at $10 per share. The commission on the single trade is $0.00 so you bought shares 10 x $10 = $100 in XYZ + $0.00 commission which adds up to $100 total cost. No commission on the trade to buy and the trade to sell means if XYZ goes up to $11 per share or $110 for your whole position, you keep all the $10 in gains if you sell.

Robinhood
Site: http://www.robinhood.com
Content: Commission Free Stock Trading
Price: Free

Direct Stock Purchase Plan (DSPP)

As with most two-sided markets, you have a buyer, a seller, and usually a middleman that brokers the deal. When buying a stock, the same is true and your broker is the middleman. Obviously, a brokerage can offer you so much more than just buying, holding, and selling the stock for you, but what if you could buy a stock without the middleman and no commissions.

Direct Stock Purchase Plans, also known as DSPPs, are a service that allows investors to buy stock direct from a company or through a transfer agent. The benefit of these services is that you can usually avoid paying commissions, but will often be restricted to certain times to buy shares and may have minimum deposits in the $100 to $500 range.

There are now hundreds of companies that permit direct stock purchases by investors. The transactions are often conducted by a transfer agent, which is a third party institution the company selling shares uses to maintain transaction records, issue stock certificates, and manage investor accounts. The company selling its shares can also be its own transfer agent, so if you have a stock you are interested in you can check with their investor relations department to see if they offer this even if you don't see one listed with a DSPP service.

There are several major agents used by DSPP participating companies to sell their shares, but one that has a large number of participating companies and has been in business for many years is Computershare.

Computershare

Started in 1978, Computershare is one of the largest direct purchase agents in the world. They represent hundreds of companies so you'll have a lot to choose from if you decide to use their service.

I personally have used Computershare with good results, but because they are a discount service, you may have to do some additional work to get your transactions completed. Overall, the whole process is pretty simple.

You'll need to visit the website and create an account

first. Once in the system, you will set up your banking details for funding purposes. Next, search for a stock you are interested in which shouldn't be hard as they represent such big names as Procter & Gamble, Exxon Mobile, Coca-Cola, Johnson & Johnson, Wal-Mart, AT&T, Ford, IBM, and many others.

After you find the stock you would like to purchase, you can go to the direct buy page, which will outline the plan details for the stock you want in a prospectus. There will be links to the official direct purchase plans from the company that will go into detail about all the fees for purchase, maintenance, and sale restrictions on the shares you purchase if there are any.

Example: Let's use The Procter & Gamble Company (Symbol: PG) a great blue-chip company that's a household name in the U.S. The direct purchase plan rules may look something like a $250 one-time purchase or $50 ongoing automatic investment from your bank once you have a Computershare account. Since you are a new investor, you may have a nominal initial setup fee but in this case, it is $0.00 for PG. Therefore, you will need to buy $250 worth of PG to get started and then purchase $50 worth per month, which is automatically purchased using your linked bank account. If the minimum amount you invest isn't enough to purchase a whole share of PG, a fractional share will be purchased.

In our example, you can see there is no cost to

purchase shares other than the money you must provide for the investment. The $250 you spent all went toward the purchase of stock, and nothing else. There may be fees and restrictions for the sale of shares so read any plan you are interested in fully. By law, all participating companies have to adhere to strict government guidelines so the fee schedule will need to be disclosed.

Once you own the stock, Computershare will keep track of your stock ownership and dividends if any are paid. If you do get paid dividends, you will have the option to reinvest the dividends into the same stock over time. This is called a Dividend Reinvestment Plan (DRIP). I cover DRIPs in Chapter 8.

Computershare
Site: http://www.computershare.com
Content: Direct Stock Purchase Plan
Price: Free (Depends on Stock Purchased)

Chapter 4. Setting Up Your Account

Submit an Application

Most brokerages I have used have a pretty standard and simplified enrollment process. The bare minimum information required by law is your name, physical address, phone number, employment status, and social security number. For the most part, account applications are done online electronically, but some brokerages may require signed paper documents to be faxed or mailed. The approval phase will vary, but I have found it takes a day or two to get your account approved once the brokerage receives the application. The next step will be to fund your account.

Funding Your Account

You have been approved to open a brokerage account so putting money in the account will be necessary before you can trade. Thankfully, this step is very easy and often a quick procedure. Once you begin the process of funding your account, the money will typically take three days to clear but can happen sooner. You will usually get a confirmation from your brokerage when the funds are available for trading.

How Much Money Do You Need?

Once you have chosen the brokerage that best meets your trading needs, you may ask, how much money do I need to fund my new account? The good news is you won't need a fortune to get started. It will depend on your brokerage's requirements, but many allow you to open a new brokerage account with no money down. You will have all the account paperwork done at that point, so you can wait until you have the money to trade with and transfer it as needed.

There is the old rule of thumb that says you don't invest any money you are not able to lose without getting into trouble. That amount will be different for everyone, but I tend to like funding my account with the minimum required by the brokerage if there is one. You can always transfer more money into your account as you get some free funds.

Another thing to remember is that many brokerages allow you to access the money in your trading account via checks and electronic transfer so if you need the money back in a pinch, you can access it fairly quickly. There also may be some interest paid on the cash balance you haven't invested which isn't a lot, but it helps. It's a good idea to read the account information carefully so you know exactly how your brokerage handles your cash position when it is not invested in stocks.

If you have a large amount of money you are putting into your trading account, you may want to ask your brokerage about using a cash management account. Cash accounts allow you to move the money into and out of your trading account quickly, but if you don't plan on investing the money for a while you can earn interest on the balance and have better control over it to pay bills or transfer to your traditional bank.

In case you are curious about whether your money in a brokerage account is protected if your brokerage becomes insolvent or goes out of business, you don't need to worry. Unlike a conventional bank account, which is insured by the Federal Deposit Insurance Corporation (FDIC) up to the allowable limit currently at $250,000 per depositor, a brokerage account is covered by another entity called the Securities Investor Protection Corporation (SIPC). The SIPC will insure your brokerage account up to $500,000 with a limit of $250,000 for uninvested cash balances. The best part is that this protection is provided free to account holders automatically just make sure the brokerage you choose is an SIPC member.

For more information about how your brokerage money is protected, visit the SIPC at http://www.sipc.org. If you would like to know more about how your money in a traditional bank account is covered, visit the FDIC at http://www.fdic.gov.

Funding Methods

There are multiple ways to fund your account, some of which are not well known to retail investors and in some cases you won't need to come up with cash. Here are some of the funding methods and how they work:

Electronic Funds Transfer (EFT)

An easy and fast way to fund your account, electronic transfer allows you to link an existing bank checking or savings account to your brokerage account which allows you to move money through the Automated Clearing House (ACH) system. Once the accounts are linked, you can often arrange for a one-time or regularly scheduled fund transfer into your trading account. It usually takes several days to complete the transfer and the service is most often free. There are usually transaction limits such as a $10 minimum and a $100,000 maximum.

This is my personal favorite funding option, but be sure to read the fine print for any EFT service. Once you have linked your brokerage with your favorite bank account, it should be easy to move money in and out of your brokerage account. This method can take around three days for the funds to clear and are available to use.

Wire Fund Transfer

Another popular money transfer method, wire transfer allows a fast and secure money transfer from one party to another. Banks often charge a fee for this convenience. With a fee of say, $10 to wire money, those costs could add up if you use it a lot. There could also be a charge from the recipient to receive the wire transfer, meaning you could pay a round-trip cost of $20 per transaction. Always read the terms for wiring money.

Cash or Check Deposit

This one is pretty obvious but many people overlook this option. Even though you are trading your own way, probably from the comfort of your own home, it is usually a good idea to develop a relationship with your brokerage and meet some of the people you could work with should you ever need help.

One of the best ways to do this is to go down the branch office or speak with the customer service team and fund your account with cash or a check. This should not cost you anything in service fees as some of the other funding methods may, but it will go a long way to making your trading experience more personal. If your brokerage doesn't have an office or one near you, don't worry, most will accept a check by mail.

Brokerage Transfer

A slightly more advanced method of funding your new brokerage account is a brokerage transfer using the stock you already own at another brokerage. Using a system called Automated Customer Account Transfer Service, or ACATS, you can arrange to have all or a specified amount of stock moved from the old account to the new one. The cost to do this is often free, but be sure to inquire first because it could cost $50 to $100 in some cases. Keep in mind that the primary benefit is that you can fund your new account without having to come up with cash, which can be difficult, especially if you have an existing brokerage account with investments you don't want to sell but want to switch to a new one. Even if there is a transaction fee to transfer your existing stocks to a cheaper brokerage, it could be worth it in the long run, since you are going to be saving a lot in commissions and other costs.

Stock Certificate Deposit

Now some of you may be thinking, did he say stock certificate, as in paper? Yes, I did. Many don't realize that it is still possible to get your stock in a paper certificate form. Though less convenient than its electronic counterpart, a paper certificate is proof you own the stock and can be given to a brokerage for deposit. Each brokerage will have its specific procedure to handle a paper certificate and due to their increasing rarity, it can be very expensive to fund your account with paper certificates.

If you already have the paper certificates, shop around for the brokerage that will do this for you for free, if possible. A better strategy may be to open an account with cash and once you have a good relationship with the brokerage, ask to transfer the paper into your account. Once you are a customer they will be more inclined to do this cheaply or waive any fees if you ask nicely.

Employee Stock Purchase Plan (ESPP)

Another way you could generate trading funds with little effort would be via your employer's stock purchase plan if you have one.

An ESPP is offered through your employer, allowing you to purchase the company's stock at regular intervals and at a significant discount. If you have this setup, the stock gets purchased and usually goes into a brokerage account. After meeting the plan requirements and once the stock is in your account, you are free to sell it and thus giving you capital to trade in other stocks. I used this trick at a former employer and didn't have to come up with any additional cash to invest as it was automatically deducted from my paycheck and the stock was purchased for me. If you aren't sure if your company offers ESPP, ask. It's a great benefit many people don't know about.

Margin Account

You will hear many opinions on if you should trade stocks with cash only or use margin to extend your buying power. The basic difference is that a margin account allows you to borrow money from your brokerage using your cash and stock as collateral versus a cash account that limits you to buying stocks using the available cash you have in your account. This can be a useful tool for an adept trader who is good at managing margin balances, but if improperly used could lead to serious financial problems.

My personal opinion for beginners is to avoid using a margin account for one simple reason. If your margined stock goes down, you could potentially owe more money than your investment. You'll also be paying an interest rate for the money you borrow, which further erodes your profits. If you stick with trading stocks on a cash basis, you will avoid any unnecessary risks and losses from an unexpected margin call or interest charges on your margin balance over time. You can always apply for a margin account with your brokerage later once you become more comfortable with trading.

Example: You want to buy a share of XYZ at $100 per share. You buy your share on margin, which means you pay only $50 that is 50 percent of the stock price requirement typical on a margin account. Unfortunately, XYZ has a disastrous quarter and the stock you own plummets to $50 per share. You lose 100 percent of your money, as you only had to pay $50 for a $100 share. You will also owe interest on the amount you borrowed. Had you bought XYZ in cash, you would have paid the full $100 but would only have lost 50 percent of your money in this example.

Funding Incentives

Get free cash! OK, this sounds too good to be true, but you really can get free cash just for opening a brokerage account. Now, it is not a sure thing, but if you time it right, you could get an incentive bonus from a brokerage for simply opening an account. As you start your research into brokerages, look for promotional deals on new accounts. In addition, they may offer you bonus cash and services for adding new funds to your existing account.

One sample offer I found allowed you to get up to $600 when opening a new account with 60 days of free trades with a minimum of a $10,000 initial deposit. That may be a large up-front cost but if you have the cash to fund your account why pass up free money?

Chapter 5. Placing Your Orders

The moment you decide to enter and exit a stock position, you control the transaction. Buying your stock at a high price, panic selling at a low price, or paying too much in commissions would decrease or eliminate your earnings potential. Enter a market order to sell on a volatile day and you could take a bath on your sale on top of your commissions. You, of course, can't control the stock's performance, but you can configure the variables of your orders to your advantage provided you know what you are doing.

Many beginning investors I speak with say when they decide to place an order they just buy and sell and aren't sure what the options are. This could be an expensive mistake. You do have options for entering your orders that give you critical tools to keep your trades from executing outside your requirements and costing you more than necessary. Depending on your brokerage, you may not have all of the order types and conditions available. Here are the main types of orders and a brief explanation of their benefits to managing your costs and losses:

Buy Orders

Buy orders are orders you place for a stock you wish to purchase. The typical buy order options for most trading platforms is ticker symbol, the number of shares, order type, and time-in-force. Once you enter the basic buy information, you place the order and it will be routed through your brokerage to the market for fulfillment. The buy will execute once your order parameters have been met. Your brokerage should then issue a trade confirmation. There are several buy order types that will determine how and when your buy orders will be executed.

Buy Market Order

Buy market orders are orders to buy a stock immediately at the best price for that stock at the time of order execution. This could be a good thing if it's a stable stock with high volume and you need the trade completed without conditions and done as soon as possible.

I personally don't use market orders much at all due to the lack of control over the execution price, I could pay more for the stock than I intended to thus make it difficult to book a profit when it comes time to sell.

Example: A stock you are watching releases an outstanding earnings report and you want to buy 100 shares quickly. You hastily enter your buy order and set it as a market order. The price is $5 a share when you place your order. Unknown to you, everyone had your idea and the buying pressure skyrockets along with the price of the stock. You get your trade confirmation but in horror, you see you paid $6 a share! After the hype fades, the stock settles back to $5 a share. You paid $600 for your 100 shares, which are now worth $500. This is a loss due to slippage or the difference in price from what you expected versus what the order filled at. Had you taken your time and entered a limit order at $5, you would have likely gotten those same shares for $100 less.

Buy Limit Order

A buy limit order lets you set a specific price to buy a stock at and a specific amount of time the order is active, referred to as time-in-force. Buy limit orders will help ensure you don't pay too much for a stock and you may even get it below your limit price, but a limit order does not guarantee the order will execute. You are assured you will only pay your limit price or lower for a stock using a buy limit order.

Buy limit orders are my primary choice for most of my buy orders. I like them because I have more control over the variables of the trade that are going to let me manage my trading costs much better. Since I try to be a disciplined trader, I don't mind waiting for my buy price and if I don't get it today, I'll wait till tomorrow.

Example: You want to buy 10 shares of XYZ and the price is holding at $11.52. Trading is slow. Your research says $11.50 is a good entry price so you put your buy limit order in at $11.50 and stick to your plan. It takes a few hours, but eventually a seller meets your price and you got the shares you wanted at the price you wanted. You have limited your risk of paying too much because the limit price prevents slippage that a market buy order could possibly have.

Sell Orders

Sell orders are orders you place for a stock you wish to sell. The typical sell order options for most trading platforms is ticker symbol, the number of shares, order type, and time-in-force. Once you enter the basic sell information, you place the order and it is routed through your brokerage to the market for fulfillment. The sell will execute quickly once your order parameters have been met and your brokerage should then issue a trade confirmation. You do have more options to put limits on your sell orders to reduce losses and fees.

Sell Market Order

Sell market orders are orders to sell a stock immediately at the best price for that stock at the time of order execution. Similar to the buy market order, this order type could lead to unnecessary losses due to your lack of control over the actual execution price. If the stock price slips downward while your market order is active, that slippage could mean you sell well below where you expected.

Example: You see some bad press about a stock you own and you want to sell. Chances are, a lot of people have the same idea. You have 100 shares at the current price of $10 per share. You enter a market order and it sells instantly. Whew, you got out in time! You check the order and wow, it sold for $9 per share and you lost $100 off the top, not to mention the commission. I never trade on emotion, but even if you are tempted to sell a stock on the down escalator know that a market order will rob you of any control you have over the price you will get and is thus a poor strategy as a general rule.

Sell Limit Order

Sell limit orders are a more controlled method of selling stock. You can select a specific number of shares to sell at a target price. Your stock will sell at your target price or better, provided the stock reaches your set price for long enough to execute the order. There is always a chance that your limit price will be reached and reverses direction without time for your trade to be filled. Because it is not a market order, you specify your sell price, but sacrifice the guarantee that your shares will sell.

Example: You decide to sell your 20 shares of XYZ when the price hits $100. You enter a day limit order to sell 20 shares at a price of $100. XYZ moves up quickly and breaks your $100 price limit quickly and the order is filled at $100.10 per share. Since a limit order will execute at your limit price or better, you made an extra $2.

Sell Stop-Loss Order

Stop-loss orders are very useful, but an often-ignored type of stock sell order designed to help you mitigate your losses. The term "stop" refers to the ability to enter the order to automatically execute a market order at or near your stop price.

Example: You own 100 shares of XYZ at $10 per share. You are only willing to lose $1 per share in value so you enter a stop-loss order for $9. If XYZ goes to $12 per share, you hold on to your shares but if XYZ falls to $9, your order will be executed at $9 or possibly below. You prevent having potentially higher losses if the stock goes well below $9 but you will not have complete control over the selling price as it will execute as a market order at the best available price once it trades at $9 or below.

Trader Tip: Be sure to set your sell price below the observed price fluctuations of your stock over time. In our example, if your stock regularly swings down to $9 and back to $10, you would want your stop loss set below $9 to prevent your sell order executing simply due to the natural movement of your stock's price.

Sell Stop-Limit Order

Like a stop-loss order, a stop-limit allows you to set a price at which you want to sell your stock, not necessarily to stop losses but to sell at your limit price. The price must reach your stop price and for long enough to execute the order. However, it doesn't guarantee your order will fill. Because the order is executed as a limit order, it will get you your limit price or perhaps better.

Example: You have 100 shares of XYZ at $20 per share. You want to sell once the price reaches $25. You enter a stop limit order for 100 shares at $25. When the XYZ target price of $25 is reached, your order converts to a limit order and will fill at your limit price of $25 or better. If the share price falls below $25 once your stop limit is converted to a day limit order, it may not execute, but at least you will not have sold below your limit price.

Sell Trailing Stop-Loss Order

Trailing stop-loss orders provide you a moving stop-loss order that adjusts (trails) to a rising stock price by increasing your sell stop as the stock price goes up. This allows for your stock to appreciate in value while giving you the peace of mind knowing if the price goes south, your sell order will execute at a certain percentage or dollar value below the market price.

Example: You own 100 shares of XYZ at $10 per share and you want to help protect your position from loss. You enter a trailing stop-loss order at 10 percent. If XYZ falls to $9, your stop-loss order will turn into a market order and sell at or near $9 preventing a larger loss if it keeps going down. If, however, XYZ goes from $10 to $20, your trailing stop loss order is still in force at 10 percent below the market price but has now moved up with the new share price. So now, with the higher price, your stop loss order will sell your stock when it drops to $18, which is 10 percent of $20. Brilliant! You locked in the upside gains, but limited your downside risk without having to watch your stock every second.

Sell Trailing Stop-Limit Order

A trailing stop limit order is a good order type when you would like to cap your maximum loss, but provide upside protection on the maximum gains. Your stop and limit price will be adjusted up as the stock price rises. If the stock price then falls to your trailing stop price, a limit order will be entered selling at the limit price or possibly better.

Example: You have 100 shares of XYZ at $30 per share and you enter a trailing stop limit order with a $1 trail amount. Your stop sell price will be $29 per share. If XYZ goes up to say, to $40 per share, your stop and limit goes up as well. Now the order will trigger when the stock price drops to $39 per share and your order will sell at limit price or perhaps better which will safeguard much of the gains.

Order Conditions

Basically, order conditions allow you to specify certain parameters of an order such as sell all, some, or none of your shares if your conditions are not met. Sometimes referred to as contingency orders, conditional orders will allow you to better control how your trade will be executed leaving less to chance.

All or None (AON)

All or None allows you to set your order to execute if all of your shares can be filled at one time. If all the specified order can't be filled, the order is canceled at the end of the trading day or time-in-force. This will save you from having to pay full commission for an order for only a fraction of the shares you intended to trade.

Example: You want to sell your 100-share position in XYZ at $10 per share but the market closes in a few minutes. You notice that XYZ is trading in 50-share lots so to prevent your order from selling just 50 of your 100 shares before market close and paying full $10 commission; you set your order to sell AON. Had you placed the order without the AON you could have had a portion of the order filled, say 50 shares, and you would pay $10 in commission. That is two percent of the sale price in commissions. Had all 100 shares sold, you would have paid only one percent of the sale value in commissions.

Time-In-Force

The Time-in-Force of your order is simply a restriction on your trade that specifies exactly how long and under what conditions it is executed or canceled. In terms of saving money, the time conditions of your order can cost you if you don't do it correctly. Here are the primary options you have to control the duration of your orders:

Day Order (Day)

As the name suggests, this type of order is only good for the day it is entered. Most often, this is the default order time duration for many trading platforms. If your order does not execute that day, it will be canceled at the end of that market day. A useful trade tool for when it's unclear where your stock is headed tomorrow.

Example: You are interested in XYZ and want 10 shares at today's low of $50, but you will be traveling and won't have access to the markets tomorrow. You hear that the company will be issuing a press release soon, but aren't sure what the market reaction will be. You enter your order to buy 10 shares at your $50 limit price as a day order. The order did not fill today and was canceled. The next day while on your trip, you see the press release caused a sell-off and the share price is now $45 per share. Had the order remained open, you could have paid your $50 per share on the way down to the new $45 price. You can now enter a new order at the lower price once you have access to your brokerage again.

Good 'til Canceled (GTC)

A Good 'til Canceled order allows you to set the target price for a stock trade and will leave that order open until it fills or when the brokerage time limit is hit. Depending on your brokerage, GTC orders could remain active for a month to perhaps six months.

In cases where a stock you are trading has low volume or a large bid to ask price difference, a GTC order allows you to set the price you want and walk away not having to watch the stock like a hawk waiting for your target price.

One important note of caution regarding a GTC order is to watch if your order gets a partial fill on one day and the remainder of the order is still active. In most cases, when a GTC order that gets partial fills on multiple days, the trade commission is charged for each day a partial fill executes. On a large order where small lots are executing over more than one trading day, it can get very expensive.

Example: You are interested in selling your 50 shares

of XYZ stock at $50 per share to generate some income soon, but won't have much time to watch your portfolio for the next few weeks. The price has been stuck at $45 per share for quite a while. You feel it will reach your sell price, but are not sure when. You enter the order to sell your 50 shares at $50 per share Good 'til Canceled and All or None protecting yourself from extra commissions for possible multiday order fills. During your hiatus from the market, you see XYZ went up to $50 and your order was eventually filled. You were able to generate the $2,500 you needed while you were away and pay only one commission.

Fill or Kill (FOK)

The name sounds deadly, but it really is a great trading tool. A Fill or Kill order must be executed immediately upon entry and in its entirety. A great way to save money for a busy trader, the fill or kill executes your order in one transaction at your price or not at all. There is no chance of trade slippage or partial fill orders thus you get exactly what you want or the order is canceled.

Example: You want to buy 10,000 shares of XYZ but you notice the order sizes today are small, so you don't want to risk only a few shares being bought, possibly increasing your trading commissions if you have to buy the rest tomorrow under a different order. You enter your order to buy 10,000 shares FOK. You have to wait a few seconds, but your brokerage is unable to match your order to a willing seller and the order is canceled.

Immediate or Cancel (IOC)

A great tool if you need to grab a stock at a specific price even if you don't get your entire order filled you will get as much of the stock as available at the price you want and any remaining shares on order will be canceled. You will avoid getting multiple trades at different prices potentially overpaying. This could be helpful in an IPO scenario, for example, and you feel the stock is going much higher you can get as much as you can immediately at your set price.

Example: XYZ Company is going public today. You have done your research and think you could make a good profit if you catch the stock near its initial IPO price of $15 per share. You want to get as many shares as you can but don't want to tie up your account balance with a standard day order. You enter an Immediate or Cancel order for 100 shares at $15 ($1,500) hoping to catch it before the market buzz drives it up. You were able to get only 50 shares filled at your price and the remainder of the order was canceled freeing up the other $750 to apply to another trade.

Order Tax Lots

It's important to know that whenever you buy shares in a stock they are categorized in lots or groups of shares which track the date, quantity, and share price for each lot for tax purposes. If you buy more of the same stock over multiple days, each lot will be of a different age and will be used to determine your capital gains tax status as well as determine what shares will sell first.

When you put your order in to sell a stock and you are not selling the whole position, your brokerage will use the default cost basis method, which usually is First In First Out or FIFO. As you begin to sell shares, the first shares bought will be the first shares sold. If the price you paid for the stock was higher in your initial lots and lower in your subsequent purchases, you can keep the gains on the newer shares by specifying the lots you want to sell when you enter the order. This will keep you from locking in losses on older shares, especially if you think the stock will go higher in the future. Sometimes it's necessary to sell some stock to cover other expenses so keep this in mind when you have multiple lots in a particular stock. Check with your brokerage to make sure it allows you to specify lots for your sell orders, it may not be easy to figure out how to do this.

Example: You want to sell 50 of your 100 shares of XYZ to free some money for another trade. Today XYZ is trading at $40 per share. You have 50 shares you bought 6 months ago at $50 per share or $2,500 total and 50 shares you bought a month ago at $30 per share or $1,500 total. If you had simply entered your order to sell 50 shares, your first lot from 6 months ago you bought at $50 would sell for $2,000. You booked a loss of $500. If you instead selected the last lot you bought at $30, you would have booked a $500 gain. So, unless you need to take a loss to offset other capital gains, why not sell the position that is actually making money.

Order Size Limits

Some brokerages have restrictions on exactly how many shares you can purchase in one order. This is not normally an issue with most stocks but if you intend to purchase an OTC stock for example, where you could potentially purchase a lot of shares, you could be limited. If you try to trade large lots, you may need to enter multiple orders to reach the amount of shares you intended to purchase incurring a commission charge for each. It may be possible to avoid this. Find out if your brokerage supports trading large lots online or to call your broker to enter one order for the entire amount.

I learned this the hard way. I once paid commission charges on 10 trades in a day to buy all the shares I wanted in a stock using my brokerage's mobile app, not knowing I could have used the website instead and entered one order for all the shares and paid commission on a single trade. D'oh!

Example: You find an interesting OTC stock that is performing well and want to buy some shares. The stock price is currently at $0.01 per share and you want to buy 100,000 shares, which would cost $1,000. You enter your order, but your brokerage has a 10,000-share limit per online order. You will need to enter 10 orders to achieve your total share goal. If your brokerage charges $10 per trade, you would pay $100 in commissions just to buy all your shares. If you want to sell, you could pay the $100 again. If you instead call your broker to buy all the shares in one order and pay the broker assist fee of $30, you would save $70, which is a good deal in that scenario.

Order Errors

Let's face it, we are only human and when inputting stock trades, it is possible to type in the wrong information. Most brokerages will have a default preview page prior to your order being submitted. Always check the order preview information to make sure it is accurate. Stupid mistakes such as entering an extra zero to an order price are sometimes called "fat finger" mistakes for obvious reasons. It has happened to me and countless others, but can be easily avoided by reviewing all your orders before placing them.

Example: You want to buy 100 shares of XYZ at $10 per share. You accidentally entered $100 as your bid price and submitted the market order in a hurry disregarding the order preview page. Your order probably won't be filled at $100 per share, but most likely it will fill and you'll pay a lot more than you wanted to. Always review your orders. Did I mention you should always review your orders?

Cancel or Modify Orders

Sometimes you enter orders only later to see you made a serious mistake. Yikes! You didn't want to buy 1000 shares of XYZ; you wanted 100. What do you do? Simple. Cancel it or modify it. I have canceled or modified many orders for various reasons over the years. Don't be afraid to cancel or modify orders if you need to. Canceling an order will actually attempt to completely remove the order if possible and modifying an order will attempt to change an existing order with your new variables. Orders are official transactions, and once submitted will sit in the system until conditions to fill or cancel are met. A market order will fill quickly, but if you entered a limit order, you may have a chance to cancel or change it even if it has been submitted. That is another good reason to use limit orders.

Depending on your brokerage, you could be charged to cancel or modify orders and the fees may not be obvious. In reality, I do not think this is common practice and I have never had to pay a cancellation or modification fee with any of the brokerages I have used. However, even if there is a charge, it may be worth it compared to the potential losses for an erroneous order being filled. Again, be sure to always review your orders prior to submission. It is your best defense against stupid mistakes. As my carpenter friends often say, "Measure twice and cut once!"

Best Times to Place Orders

Regular Market Hours

Standard market hours in the United States are 9:30 am to 4 pm EST Monday through Friday. Generally speaking, the best time to trade stocks is during normal market hours. The volume, price, and liquidity for stocks are best during this time. Compared to extended hours trading, you can stand the best chance of preventing excess costs due to uncontrollable trading risks inherent to trading outside the normal market day.

Extended-Hours Trading

Once only available to institutional players, after-hours trading is now available to many retail investors.

Extended-hours trading is generally defined as trading from 8 am to 9:30 am and from 4 pm to 6:30 pm EST but could be different depending on the market. Sometimes referred to as after-hours, or AH trading, it also has an alternate nickname, "amateur hour", relating to the greater risk and chances an individual investor could get in trouble during this time. Because there is typically less volume in extended hour trading, it is more difficult to trade during this time and you may pay more for your stock depending on your order conditions.

Risks associated with extended-hours trading include lower liquidity, higher volatility, unlinked markets, press releases, and a wider pricing spreads. Because of the greater risks, your brokerage may prohibit you from trading AH or have you use a broker to place the order for you costing you more for the trade.

Example: A stock you have been watching has had a pullback this week to $5 per share and you are ready to buy. The market closes and you see the company issues a stellar press release and you're sure the stock is going way up tomorrow. The price after market is up to $6 already so you want to buy before it goes much higher in the morning. Your brokerage requires you to have a representative place the AH order for a fee of $30 so you call and tell him to buy 100 shares at $6 market order. You get your after-hours order filled at $6.20 per share. You paid $620 for your shares and $30 in broker fees, or $650 for your total order. The next morning, the market normalizes and the stock is back down to $5 since investors were not as excited about the news release as the after-hours traders. If you normally have $10 trade commissions, you could have gotten your 100 shares for $510 had you waited to buy the following day during regular market hours.

Best Days to Trade Stocks

Did you know there are good days and bad days to trade your stocks? I didn't know this until I read some interesting studies about it. It is sometimes called Calendar Effect and might be helpful when planning your trades.

In one study titled, *"The Day of the Week Effect on Stock Market Volatility"* published by The Journal of Economics and Finance (Kiymaz & Berument, 2001), researchers reviewed S&P 500 data covering several decades from 1973 to 1997. They found that calendar anomalies provide interesting insight on which days might be best to trade. For example, attributed to the Day of the Week Effect, Mondays have been statistically down days during bull market periods, possibly giving traders better buying opportunities. Conversely, Wednesdays often perform well and could be good days to sell stock.

Chapter 6. Protecting Gains

The whole point of buying a stock is the end result of making a profit. One of the most common mistakes investors make is to not take profits when they have the chance. These traders probably aren't using a trade plan but even if you know your stock's exit price, what other factors should you consider? What if one of your investments goes up faster than you planned? What will the tax liability be? What do you do with the extra money once you have captured it? These are all very good questions and I want to present some basic but very important strategies to not only maximize the gains you have but to safeguard them and the rest of your cash so you will be able to keep trading.

Capital Gains

There are two ways to classify your stock positions for tax purposes. Stock you own 12 months or more (long-term) and stock you own for less than 12 months (short-term). Whether your stocks are in a long-term capital gain position or short-term capital gains position there are different strategies to maximize and retain your earnings.

Long-Term

The federal government considers your stock as "long" for tax purposes after you have held your shares for 12 months or longer. This means that you now qualify for long-term capital gains. This is really a big deal because your capital gains tax rate goes from being at your standard income tax rate to being taxed at a reduced long-term capital gains rate, which is intended to encourage people to invest in companies for the long haul. Depending on your regular income the difference in tax rates can be very significant.

Example: You make $60,000 per year at your day job. Your standard simple tax rate is say 25 percent and the estimated long-term capital gains rate for you is at 15 percent. You have 100 shares of XYZ you got at $5 per share, costing you $500. You hold the stock for 11 months and sell for $10 per share ($1,000), giving you gains of $500 on top of your original investment. Your standard tax rate total would be $125. Nevertheless, if you held that stock for one more month and sold, your long-term capital gains rate would be 15 percent or $75! I don't know about you, but I sure would love to keep $50 on one trade simply by waiting a little longer.

Short-Term

The second way to classify your stock position is short-term often referred to as "short". Not to be confused with "short selling" a stock or betting a stock is going down, "short" is when the government has not deemed your position long-term yet and is not subject to the lower capital gains tax rate. You know the tax benefit of holding a stock for 12 months, but what if your stock catches a rocket ride in month one and you are looking at a 30 percent gain in a short-term position.

I know I have had stocks in my portfolio that experienced an unexpected rise and appreciated by far more than I anticipated. At first, that would seem like a great problem to have but often traders get a little greedy and say, "It's going to the moon. I'm holding!" Maybe it keeps going up or maybe not, but the reality is, you have gains on the table and if you don't sell at least some of your position, it's just a paper gain. My general rule of thumb is that if I have a stock that goes up significantly in the short-term, I'll sell a portion of my position locking in some of the gains. If it goes higher over a year, great, I'll sell more and pay less in taxes.

One major short-term trading benefit is compounding. In a nutshell, compounding is when a stock you sell generates gains, you then reinvest those gains, and they earn their own gains.

Caution: This can be dangerous if you don't manage your trade commissions, taxes, and trade prices properly. The goal is to buy low then sell high enough to cover your short-term taxes and trade costs with enough left over to reinvest. Research this thoroughly or discuss it with a financial advisor before you decide if this strategy is right for you.

Example: You invest $1,000 in XYZ Corporation and it appreciates by 10 percent or a $100. You sell the stock, locking in your gains and now you have $1,100 to reinvest. Your new stock goes up by the same 10 percent, but now you have $110 in gains. Repeat this often enough and you can continually compound your investment more so than had you bought and sold once. Repeat this compounding over many years and that is how millionaires are made. The added benefit of doing this would be to potentially generate more money than would be saved in holding a position long for 12 months and getting the lower capital gains rate one time.

Price Catalysts

I'm sure you have heard of a pharmaceutical company that got FDA approval for a blockbuster drug and the stock made a parabolic rise up or a darling restaurant stock that tanked when they had a rash of food illness cases. These are examples of catalysts.

Catalysts as illustrated above can be good or bad and can also include analyst opinions, earnings reports, lawsuits, hostile takeovers, etc.

On the buying side, if a stock you are thinking of

getting a position in has a negative catalyst that isn't a fundamental problem with the company, you might consider buying at that time. Often, stocks recover their losses if the catalyst is just a hiccup with an unreasonable reaction from the market.

On the selling side, a stock you own has a positive catalyst that puts significant gains on the table that would be a great time to sell a portion of your position to capture that money before the trend reverses. As a disciplined investor, you will already have a stock price set when you want to sell and once your stock reaches it, you stick to your plan. An old saying goes, "No one ever got hurt by taking profits." I certainly agree with that.

Price Targets

Later in this book, you will see the power of a trading journal and trade plan, which are very useful tools to track your buy and sell prices. Once those prices are reached you need to stick to your plan and execute the order. It is a practice I always try to stick with and it creates a good habit that helps me stay focused.

Buying

Your exact entry price will be a price you derive from your analysis and trade strategy, but when planning to buy a stock set the price low enough to allow for a decent gain but not so low you will not get your order filled.

You should never be emotional about buying a stock and chase the price up, especially when the stock is moving up quickly. As you learned earlier, the limit order is a tool you should be using to reduce risk. By putting in a limit order to buy your stock at your price it will either get filled if it hits that price or not. If it does not, you saved your money for another day of trading. Stocks go up and stocks go down if you missed the price run don't worry review your plan and try again.

Selling

When planning your selling price target, set the price high enough to make enough money to be profitable being sure to factor in your round-trip trading costs. This is a common rookie mistake as it's easy to forget about your trading commissions when calculating your gains.

Additionally, remember the old trading adage, "Pigs get fat, but hogs get slaughtered!" An easy way to keep your plans on track is to set a sell order for your stock at the exact price you wish to sell right after you buy it. Once the sell order is in the system, you will increase the chances of your order being filled if it hits your set price target when it occurs even if you are not watching your brokerage account. Computers aren't emotional so a limit order won't care how excited you are about your winning position, the order gets filled automatically and you get your gains and a little fatter.

Trader Tip: Set up price alerts for all the stocks you own and the ones you plan on buying. This is a very simple yet powerful tool allowing you to get immediate price notifications by text message or email. Instead of watching all your stocks all the time, you will know when it is time to closely monitor the stocks that approach your target prices. All the brokerages I use have this feature and if yours doesn't, many of the stock sites I mentioned offer it for free.

Saving Gains

Another good strategy to guard some of your trading gains is to move the money to a separate bank account. I got in the habit of taking a percentage of my earnings out of my trading account and moving it to an interest bearing bank account with a separate institution. It was a wise move. Doing this removes the temptation to immediately invest that money again giving you another layer of self-control. You can always move the money back into your trading account, but it will take more effort. Let the euphoria of success subside and apply your discipline to your new trade plan.

In addition to protecting some of your earned cash, it will allow you to plan better for tax time. Investors who fail to take out gains to cover their taxes can have a hard time coming up with the money when it's time to pay. When you sell a stock with a gain, make sure to remove the money to cover your taxes. This is a great habit to adopt. I like to transfer that money into my savings account once the funds settle from the sale of a stock, which is typically three days due to regulations.

Caution: You will need to consult with your accountant, but generally, the taxes on the profits from selling stock are due in the fiscal quarter they are sold. I mentioned the various federal tax rates previously, but this is the time you need to also account for your state and local taxes as well. One of the most common reasons people do not pay their taxes is because they just don't have the money. Why give the government a reason to come calling on you.

Chapter 7. Managing Risk

Now that you have seen some of the ways to cut costs and protect gains, what about managing some of the other risks associated with trading stocks?

I can't overstate the fact that trading stocks is risky. Ask any professional skydiver, skier, or motorcyclist if what they do has risks and they will likely say yes, but they learned how to manage them with training and practice. Trading risk can be managed but never eliminated completely. You will learn your own methods for risk control, but here are a few critical areas you can start with:

Controlling Emotions

Ask a seasoned trader what are the skills that keep him from losing money and making dumb decisions and you will likely find controlling emotions and discipline are at the top of his list. A common investing saying goes, "Scared money doesn't make money." That is often true, however, overconfidence and unbridled excitement can cost you if you fail to take profits when you have the chance.

Discipline is the glue that holds your trading plans together. Without it you will be swayed by irrelevant events or tempting distractions that would cause you to make irrational decisions. An undisciplined investor doesn't perform proper due diligence, take notes, or stick to his plans. "Plan your trade and trade your plan" is the mantra of a successful trader. With attention deficit on the rise, it takes an effort to maintain a cool head and solid game plan.

Trading Journal

A trading journal sounds like extra work to some, but to savvy traders, it is a critical component of their strategy for success. Much like an accountant will keep a ledger of sales and expenses for a company's business, a trading journal will allow you to keep accurate records of your trades and gives you the ability to track your progress over time and see which of your strategies worked and which ones didn't.

Depending on your work style you can either keep a trade journal on paper, which can offer a more tangible record of your trading, or you can use an electronic spreadsheet that is far more flexible and powerful in being able to search, sort data, and generate reports showing exactly what data you want over any time frame you want. Whichever format you decide to use, it is important to incorporate it into your daily routine. Good habits will help you keep the discipline necessary to achieve your trading goals.

Just what does a trading journal look like? It varies
from trader to trader, but some key information is
required to give you enough data to make it useful. Some
things you want to track are the stock symbol, entry price,
entry date, exit price, exit date, trade commissions, and
whether the trade was a gain or a loss. It's important to
also include space for your notes for each of your stock
trades. This is the place you will note your thoughts on
why you bought the stock, what price you expect to sell
the stock, and any company events you are expecting to
see. In general, keep track of any information regarding
each trade that will help you learn from your mistakes
and highlight your successes. Knowing is half the battle
so once you figure out what works and what doesn't
work you can do more of what is making you money and
less of what costs you.

Trade Plan

One more very helpful trading tool that pushes you
to maintain discipline when it comes to actually trading
your stocks is a trade plan. This is a simple list of as much
quantifiable information on a trade that you can compile.
Include critical data about the market, stock, price,
strategy, investment capital, and the trade itself. The more
reasons you can document to justify a decision to trade a
stock will help you remove your emotional attachment
and give you a better chance of making money and

avoiding potential losses.

A trade plan is intended to provide solid evidence of your trade's validity. No guessing allowed. I think of it as a job interview for a trade I'm considering. Is this one going to work out or is it time to move on to the next candidate?

Planning to trade should become second nature. Write this down, "Failing to plan is planning to fail." As with anything, planning is critical to trading stocks. I like to keep a watch list of all the stocks I am interested in. I'll watch the stocks over time and figure out what my entry price will be and if I do buy it, what my exit price will be. I keep all that data updated daily in my trade plans. When it comes time to buy, I already know what price I want to pay and when I want to sell based on my own research. I also know what my costs to trade that stock will be and a general idea of my tax rates so I can properly calculate my numbers.

A trade plan may seem silly to a new trader, but this is one of the simplest ways to limit the risks and limit your potential losses before you trade a stock. If you fail to properly screen a stock, you are only gambling with your money. Even stock speculators use some form of a checklist before they trade stocks and will refrain from making blind trading decisions.

Book Buyer Bonus: As a thank you for buying this

book, I have authorized exclusive access to a FREE *Trade Planner*. Simply visit the link below to get your copy. This guide will give you a flexible template for creating your own custom trade plans that work best for you. Enjoy!

http://www.tradestockscheap.com/trade-plan

Money Management

Money management is perhaps the greatest skill you can develop to achieve your stock trading goals. Managing your money is something you are probably already doing to some degree, but here are a few key concepts to help keep your brokerage account in good financial shape:

Paper Trading

If you are not confident with your stock trading, a great strategy to hone your skills is to try paper trading first. This takes all the financial risk out of your trading, but gives you the functionality of a real brokerage account. You can test all your trade ideas buying and selling according to your trade plans. The more you go through the motions of trading, the more confidence you will develop over time.

A paper trading system or simulator works much the

same way a live trading account does, but it is not using real money. You will typically be given a virtual cash balance to conduct your virtual trading. The best free trading simulator I have used is from Investopedia.

Go to http://www.investopedia.com/simulator and register. Once registered, you will be taken to the paper trading system and be able to select from multiple "games'" which allow you to trade in competition with other members. Once in your account, you'll see your virtual cash balance, portfolio, and links to the simulator tutorials. Trading is permitted during regular market hours just as a live system so you're sure to get a realistic trading experience minus the risk.

If you want to choose another simulator, there are also brokerages that offer a virtual trading platform to their account holders. E*TRADE and thinkorswim® are two of the most popular.

Trader Tip: I highly encourage anyone who is not established in stock trading to get set up with a paper trading account. You will be free to experiment and learn about trading in a safe, risk-free environment building confidence as you go. Sadly, I discovered these late in my trading life and boy they could have saved me money and frustration. I still use them to test new strategies or get my confidence up if I haven't traded in a while.

All-In Trading

It is important to never use all your trading funds towards a single trade. Let me say that again. It is important to never use all of your trading funds toward a single trade. It may be tempting to want to go all-in on a favorite stock when the price is moving up, but that is a really bad idea. A general guide is to not commit any more than say two percent of your investment capital or less in one particular trade. It is a basic risk management strategy that helps account for the dreaded worst-case scenario. If a disaster ever occurred and the stock you bought crashes, you only lost a small percentage of your total capital, allowing you to trade another day and attempt a recovery.

Diversification

A critical aspect of trading-risk management is to keep your portfolio diversified. Depending on whom you talk to, diversification can mean different things, but in general, don't put all your money in one stock or market sector. Diversification planning also includes investing in different asset types, different markets, and at different times in your life. For the purposes of this book, I only use stocks as an example. Research or speak to a financial professional for the full story and benefits of diversification.

Sometimes called correlated assets, owing similar stocks exposes you to avoidable risks. If you have $1,000 to invest, don't buy $1,000 worth of one stock or market sector. As a general example, no more than, say 10 percent of your money would be in any one stock or sector. Therefore, with your $1,000 you could buy $100 worth of 10 different stocks and not all in a single sector.

You may like the pharmaceutical space, but even if you buy 10 different pharmaceutical stocks, you are not really diversified as those stocks are all in the same market sector. If the pharmaceutical sector crumbles, all of your 10 stocks will likely go down at the same time.

This is just a crude example to illustrate the point on diversification. There are whole books dedicated to investment diversification, learn as much as you can about it.

Personal Discipline

Your habits also play a significant role in risk management. Just because you can trade stocks from home doesn't mean it's a leisure activity. On days I plan to trade stocks, I always get a good night's sleep, get up early (usually an hour before the markets open), eat a good breakfast, clean up my desk, turn the phone ringer off, and plan out my day. If you take yourself seriously, you will take your trading seriously and develop a good work ethic. You will be less likely to make stupid mistakes or trade out of fear if you are clear-headed, focused, and dedicated. The times I made panic sales or bought stocks for way too much were always on days where my head was not in the right place.

Trader Tip: Do not feel like you have to trade every day. Even diehard day traders take days off if they don't feel things are going well. It could be that you have something on your mind or the market is so unpredictable you can't figure it out. Regardless of why things aren't right, trust your instincts and sit the day out. There is always another day and another opportunity, patience will pay off in the trading world.

Trader Education

Even after trading for years and reading countless books on trading and investing, I still learn new things every day. I try to read one new investing-related article a day at the minimum. I never assume I know everything about anything so I keep an open mind and admit if I don't know something. There will always be things you don't know you don't know so do your best to learn and enjoy the experience.

I chose brokerages that offer excellent tools and educational materials and I encourage you to consider that when choosing your brokerage. They will often have good tutorials on how their specific brokerage system works so you can familiarize yourself with the platform you will be using the most.

To supplement your brokerages' educational offering, I have found a few great stock trading and investing resources that offer sound information that I recommend and hope you find useful:

SEC Beginners' Investing Guide
https://www.sec.gov/investor/pubs/begininvest.htm

Provided by the Office of Investor Education and Advocacy, the Investors Beginners' Guide covers a host of common topics such as investments, cost calculators, research ideas and much more, all for free.

Investopedia University
http://www.investopedia.com/university

As with everything at Investopedia, the University section contains a bevy of free professionally done guides and videos of many trading and investing topics. I have spent countless hours here educating myself and I hope you do too.

Morningstar Investing Classroom®
http://www.morningstar.com/cover/classroom.html

A more formalized training setting, the Morningstar® Investing Classroom, is a great place to go to trading school. You'll be able to choose your curriculum focusing on what areas you want to study most. You can learn at your own pace by taking short quizzes, which allow you to accumulate credits you can later apply toward a premium subscription. The courses are entertaining, educational, and free.

Professional Help

As an individual investor, you are looking to do it all yourself, entering your own trades, managing your money, researching, and preparing your own tax returns. It's an admirable goal to be independent, but trading stocks is a serious business and you want good professionals to back you up and provide expertise in areas in which you aren't proficient.

Here are a few of the people you should consider adding to your team. The more trained professionals you can have to share ideas with and ask questions of, the better you can execute sound strategies and help keep you from making costly mistakes you could have avoided.

Stockbroker

I hope you did a good amount of research when choosing your brokerage. Even though you are saving money entering your own orders there is that time you will need help. It's a good idea to visit your local brokerage branch if there is one nearby. If your brokerage doesn't have a customer service office, call or email a representative and get familiar with their team. You can learn a lot about your brokerage just by how their customer service works. Good stockbrokers are knowledgeable, courteous, and helpful.

Establishing a personal relationship with a representative who knows who you are and what your goals are will give them more incentive to help in a pinch. Moreover, it is just good practice to learn all you can about trading so treat it as a learning experience. Your stockbroker should not charge for contacting him or stopping by, you aren't asking him to or perform a billable task. You will make valuable contacts at your brokerage and that is well worth the effort.

Certified Public Accountant (CPA)

They say a person who is his own lawyer has a fool for a client. There is some wisdom in that and I tend to believe that has some truth in being your own accountant as well. I know a lot of people who take pride in doing their own taxes and saving a few dollars; I used to be one of them. I certainly don't blame them, but if you are trading stocks, you could be costing yourself more money than you are saving.

Not only does trading stock change your income tax and possibly your tax due dates, but it increases the complexity of your tax return. Since time is money, you could be better off having an accountant handle the time-consuming task of tax preparation so you can spend more time planning your trades.

It's important to know that all CPAs are accountants, but not all accountants are CPAs. Why does this matter? A CPA must meet a higher standard of examination, education, experience, and ethics. In fact, CPAs must undergo one of the toughest professional exams around. To make sure they stay sharp and up to date, a CPA will need to complete Continuing Professional Education (CPE) to remain certified. A CPA license is issued by the individual states or territories in the United States so finding one in your local area means he will also be well versed in the local tax codes that apply to you.

In many cases, you would be spending several hundred dollars for a CPA to prepare your itemized individual tax return, but that could be easily offset by the maximized deductions and peace of mind they offer.

When searching for a CPA, take the time to meet with him. A good CPA will provide a complimentary consolation and look forward to meeting you in person. The best way I have found a CPA is by word of mouth from someone I trust. You want someone you can build a relationship with. Evaluate his credentials, reputation, breadth of services, availability, familiarity with stock trading, and whether he is a good fit with your personality. The CPA will often be able to provide much more help than just tax preparation and will become a trusted member of your success team.

If you are having a hard time finding a CPA in your area or would like to learn more about CPAs and taxes, the American Institute of CPAs has an excellent consumer resource section. There you can find a CPA, review their specialties, and even see if there were any disciplinary actions against them. It's a good place to start and I found their tax education resources very useful.

AICPA
http://www.aicpa.org/ForThePublic/Pages/ForthePublic.aspx

Registered Investment Adviser (RIA)

Depending on your wealth level, self-discipline, or trading aptitude, you may want additional help with your investing. A Registered Investment Adviser (RIA) gives you one more professional on your side guiding your choices and helping you make and grow your investment money. As a trader, you will often be focused on the details of daily trade strategies, but an investment adviser will meet with you regularly to determine if you are moving towards your long-term goals and making the proper investments for your risk tolerance and life circumstances.

Unlike some less regulated financial professionals, an RIA is bound by a fiduciary standard mandated by the U.S. Investment Advisers Act of 1940. This is a key benefit and requires them to recommend investments that are in your best interests not what makes them money. As I stated earlier, they may be a good option, especially if you aren't willing or able to put in the time and effort to manage your investment portfolio. The added expense could be burdensome and unnecessary if you are the organized and financially literate type. A good accountant can often help you with much of the financial planning and that may be good enough.

If you are interested in finding an RIA, check with friends and family for a trusted recommendation. If you do not find an RIA you like, you can find a wealth of information at the SEC's Investment Adviser Public Disclosure (IAPD) website.

IAPD
http://www.investor.gov/researching-managing-investments/working-investment-professionals/brokers-advisors/research-advisor

There you can review the RIA's fees, conduct, conflicts of interest, affiliations, disciplinary actions, and much more. After you find a few RIAs you like in your area, plan time to meet with them until you find the right fit for your investment needs and personality. As with other professionals on your team, you want to build a long-term relationship with a reputable RIA that is interested in you and your needs.

Initial consultations should be free, so don't be afraid to shop around and find the best fit for you. Some RIAs will not work with smaller clients, but many do. Always ask about how much they charge, what they charge for, and if they invest in the stocks they recommend. An RIA should be upfront about all this. It is your money, you want the best service at the best price or you take your business elsewhere.

Chapter 8. More Money Saving Ideas

Dividend Stocks

A public company that distributes some of its earnings to its shareholders is called a dividend stock. Dividend stocks are a great way to put money back in your account just for owning the stock. The dividends are typically distributed on a quarterly basis and you are paid the dividend for each share of the stock you own. I like to have trade strategies and investment strategies and one of my favorite investment strategies is to own some well-performing dividend stocks.

Example: You buy 100 shares of XYZ and its dividend is $.50 per share. If the dividend payment schedule is quarterly, every 3 months as long as you hold the stock, you get paid $50. The dividend will normally be deposited into your trading account. Once you have the dividend, you can either reinvest or hold it in your cash position. Getting that dividend is always a good feeling and rewards you for making a sound financial decision.

Dividend Reinvestment Plan (DRIP)

If you own a dividend paying stock, that dividend money is deposited into your brokerage account and it becomes an asset for you to use. You can either take it out to use or reinvest it. DRIPs are a way for a shareholder to specify how much and when your dividend funds from a stock get applied to purchase more shares of that same stock over time.

Dividend reinvestment can be used as part of a long-term investment strategy. Reinvesting dividends over time could really add up. One of the key parts is the process can be entirely automated so you don't have to think about it once you are enrolled in the plan. Be smart, as you have learned everything has fine print and DRIPs are no exception. There could again be hidden fees to reinvest your dividend money. It is ok to automate the reinvestment process, but the final decision to reinvest or not should be a conscious one. You want a plan that allows you to opt-out if you don't want to do it and without penalty.

DRIPs can be offered through your brokerage and are often part of the Direct Purchase Plans, which I covered earlier. Dividends are obviously considered income so they are also taxed. Be sure to know your tax liability.

Example: You own 1,000 shares of XYZ a popular dividend paying stock. Your quarterly dividend is $0.25 per share. Every quarter you get $250 deposited into your brokerage account. You were smart and enrolled in the DRIP and apply those dividends automatically to buy more XYZ. So provided the dividend stays the same each quarter, you will be earning $1,000 in dividends and purchasing another $1,000 worth of XYZ stock this year. The best part is all of the new shares will all be earning their own dividends so next year the dividend payout should increase.

Referral Programs

Another great way to get extra money into your trading account with little effort is by getting your brokerage to pay you for referring people to open an account with it. Once you have your trading account and it is a service you like, why wouldn't you talk to those you know about it?

One offer currently running at a popular discount brokerage is get three free trades for every person you refer who opens up a qualifying account. With a trade commission of $10, that is $30 free just for referring someone. That's a no-brainer.

Active Trading Rewards

There may come a time when you find yourself trading more often. Perhaps you are really getting the hang of it moving towards a trading career. I know I had no intention of making a lot of trades when I first started, but eventually, I did. If this happens, take advantage of the possible benefits.

Some brokerages will upgrade your account and offer better services and pricing if you meet their criteria for an active trader. Check with your brokerage if they offer this, as it may not be an advertised benefit.

Caution: Active trading should not be confused with day trading. If you start trading a lot daily, you may change the classification of your account and its funding requirements. Your account could be flagged as a Pattern Day Trade account if you make more than four day trades (buy and sell the same stock) during five business days. If this happens, you will be subject to a $25,000 account balance minimum, which must be maintained at all times.

A day trade is simply buying and selling the same stock during the same trading day. If you buy 10 different stocks in a single day, but don't sell them that day, they aren't considered day trades.

Tax Loss Harvesting

I am not an accountant and I am not giving tax guidance here, but one money-saving strategy I have used is to book a loss from an under-performing stock in a given tax year to help offset my capital gains tax burden. It seems counterintuitive to lock in a loss, but this could be a helpful tool. If you already have taxable gains from other stocks you sold this year, the loss will reduce your taxes for those winning trades. At the time of this writing, the basic limit to a stock loss in a tax year is $3,000 and if your loss is in excess of that, you can carry that forward to following tax years. If you don't already have one, I discuss the benefits of having a good accountant in Chapter 7. A good accountant should know about this tax strategy and could advise you on its proper use.

Free Stock

We live in the age of crazy promotions and clever start-up ideas that really push the envelope of sanity. If you had the chance to get in on the ground floor of a future IPO before it was famous, wouldn't you want in?

I learned a valuable lesson when I took advantage of an offer to earn free shares in a now public travel company when it was a little start-up. I got eight shares for referring friends to their site. I got a share for every person I referred who visited and opened an account with the company. I eventually received instructions on how to register my shares and that was it. A few years later, the company went public and soared in price. I took the paperwork to my brokerage and the shares appeared in my account.

I still see these offers from time to time. If it appears legitimate and interesting to you, jump on it. Who knows! You may get a few shares of a future superstar.

Chapter 9. Summary

I want to commend you on making it to the end. We have covered a lot of ideas and concepts so here is a quick recap of the key points I hope you take away from this book.

Best Brokerage

Find the right brokerage that lets you trade for less, provides good research tools, education, and customer service. This is going to save you time, money, and frustration over the years. Even if you already have a brokerage but want to switch to a better one, don't hesitate. I have used many brokerages over the years and now trade with the ones that save me money and I like the most. You are the customer don't settle for mediocre.

Due Diligence

Do all your own research. I can't stress that enough. If you follow a stranger's recommendation blindly, you don't know his intentions or competence. You will not own the mistake if things go wrong and it will be harder to learn from it.

The less time you have to educate yourself on stocks,

the fewer stocks you should trade. If you have one hour a week to fully research a trade idea, only commit to that one trade. Having 10 stocks in your portfolio and not knowing why you own them is foolish. Don't be foolish. I would rather own one stock that I knew everything about and could explain to anyone who asks why I own it.

The exception would be if you choose to use an RIA. They are regulated professionals and are working on your team. Even though you are following their advice you should ask questions and study the investment strategies they recommend, you will learn a lot over time.

Proper Planning

Remember to trade with purpose. Always know why you are buying and why you are selling a stock. There is never a need to trade for the fun of it. You are in the business of making money and when you trade stocks based on emotions or whims, you will make mistakes. If you can't control your emotions, you will lose money and should probably rethink trading stocks.

Eternal Education

Your education should never stop. Don't fall victim to complacency or over confidence in your trading. You may get lucky with one strategy or stock pick and feel like you figured it out. I have often felt that way only to lose my shirt on the next trade I made. Just when you think you know how trading works, you find out something else you didn't know. Use a trading journal and log your successes and failures and one day you might write your own book on stock trading. It's a journey, not a destination. Enjoy it and embrace the lessons that come your way. You will make mistakes, but don't be too hard on yourself. Learn why you made the mistake and don't do that again. I have provided many good sources for stock trading and investing information in this book, but that is just the beginning. I want you to exceed the limits of what I shared with you here.

Risk Reduction

One of my favorite quotes pertaining to stock trading is from Warren Buffett, who said, "Rule No. 1: Never lose money. Rule No. 2 is never forget Rule No. 1." The message is priceless and I think it encapsulates the spirit of this book. Protect your money, it's the lifeblood of your trading.

Whether you are trading a stock, transferring funds, or paying for trading information be clever and always look for the best, safest, and least expensive solution that meets your needs. Do <u>not</u> take unnecessary chances. If you are careless, unmotivated, and unprepared you will lose money in the stock market. You know better than that now. <u>Limiting your risks will help limit your losses.</u>

I wish you the very best in your trading endeavors. Stay calm, be smart, and make money. Good Luck!

Glossary Of Terms

Like any large, highly technical industry, stock trading has a huge amount of slang, acronyms, abbreviations, and terms specific to it. If I said OTC, L2, Ask, Long, or Market Maker would you know what I was talking about? Even if you are a long-time trader and just read this book you may still have terms you aren't familiar with. Knowing this, I wanted to define some key terms I use in my own words. I distilled the definitions down to pertain to trading stocks and my use of the terms in this book.

I'd like to give special thanks to Investopedia http://www.investopedia.com and the Securities and Exchange Commission http://www.sec.gov/investor for their tremendous help in researching this book.

These sites are outstanding resources for any trader. I have them bookmarked and I will reference them whenever I have a trading term I don't understand. I encourage you to get in the habit of researching any trading concept you don't know much about. You'll be a better trader for it.

Trader Tip: Investopedia has a Term of the Day email newsletter that I highly recommend. You will learn a new investment related term every day to help continue your trading education for free.

Analysis – The evaluation of stocks based on a predetermined set of inputs to determine the state of the equity. Some examples are fundamental, technical, quantitative, and qualitative.

Analyst – A professional person or service with expertise in stocks that issues recommendations such as sell, buy, or hold and often charges for their detailed analyst reports.

All or None (AON) – A condition that a stock order is filled for the total amount of shares in the order or the order is not executed, but could be open for a specified duration.

Ask – The ask refers to the price a seller is willing to sell a stock for and the amount of shares being offered for sale.

Automated Customer Account Transfer Service (ACATS) – A service that conducts transfers of investors securities from one account to another.

Bear Market – A market condition when stock prices are falling.

Bid – The bid refers to the price a buyer is willing to

pay for a stock and the amount of shares being sought for purchase.

Brokerage (Broker) – A brokerage is the company offering an investor the access to a trading platform to trade stocks and can also provide access to a stockbroker who can assist an investor with making trades.

Bull Market – A market condition when stock prices are rising.

Capital Gains (Gains) – The money made off the increase in the price of a stock.

Cash Management Account – An account similar to a traditional bank account that is hosted with your brokerage to facilitate the management of your cash.

Chart – A graphical display of various elements of a stock's performance over a specified time period.

Commission – A fee charged by a broker to handle the buying or selling of a stock on behalf of an investor.

Contingency Order – An order that has specific rules applied to it that must be met in order to execute.

Day Order (DAY) – An order to buy or sell a stock that will be canceled at the end of that trading day.

Day Trader– An individual investor who buys and sells stocks multiple times in a single trading day.

Direct-Access Trading (DAT) – A trading system allowing for the trading of stock directly with the markets without using a broker.

Diversification– The practice of spreading the risk of investing by buying stocks in different markets and sectors to help prevent overinvesting in any one area.

Dividend – A distribution to a shareholder of part of a public company's earnings determined by the board of directors at a regular interval such as quarterly.

Dividend Reinvestment Plan (DRIP) – A plan provided by a public company or brokerage to reinvest a shareholders' dividends on a regular basis.

Dollar Cost Averaging (DCA) – An investing strategy of buying a specified amount of stock on a set schedule over time, regardless of the stock price at the time of purchase.

Due Diligence (DD) – A sufficient level of evaluation conducted by an investor to determine if an investment is a sound one.

Duration Order – Any order to buy or sell stock that has a specified length of time to execute associated with it.

Electronic Funds Transfer (EFT) – A transfer of funds electronically directly from a trader's bank account to their brokerage account.

Electronic Communication Network (ECN) – A system used to match stock buyers and sellers together and made accessible to an investor through a brokerage's website or trading application.

Equity – A financial instrument of ownership in a public company usually represented by a share of stock.

Employee Stock Purchase Plan (ESPP) – An employer managed stock purchase program allowing employees to purchase shares in the company over time at a discounted rate.

Exchange – A market to exchange the ownership of stock between sellers and buyers such as the New York Stock Exchange (NYSE).

Execution (Execute) – The completion of an order to buy or sell a stock alternately used for the term fill.

Federal Deposit Insurance Corporation (FDIC) – The government agency charged with protecting consumers' bank deposits in the case of bank insolvency.

Fill – The execution or fulfillment of an order to buy or sell a stock.

Fill-or-Kill (FOK) – An order condition to buy or sell all of the specified shares immediately or it is killed (canceled).

First In, First Out (FIFO) – A common share management strategy that sells the shares bought first before selling shares bought at a later date.

Fractional Share – A share of stock that is a fraction of one whole share associated commonly produced by dividend reinvestment plans when not enough money is present to purchase a full share of that stock.

Good 'til Canceled (GTC) – An order condition that keeps the order open until the trade executes, expires, or is canceled.

Immediate or Cancel (IOC) – An order condition where all or a portion of an order is filled immediately or canceled.

Index – A representative group of securities reflecting the state of a segment of the stock markets.

High-Frequency Trading (HFT) – An electronic trading system designed to complete orders quickly, at the best prices, and increasing market liquidity.

Interactive Voice Response System (IVR) – An automated phone ordering system allowing a trader to place trades without the need for a broker or online trading system.

Investor – An individual who uses her money in stocks with the intention of making money on those investments.

Investor Relations (IR) – A department in a company responsible for handling issues investors have related to the company's stock.

Initial Public Offering (IPO) – A private company's first issuance of stock to the public for purchase.

Level I (Level 1, L1, L I, Li) – A basic stock price quote that lists the last price and volume of shares exchanged which is either real-time or delayed.

Level II (Level 2, L2, L II, Lii) – A detailed real-time stock price quote that shows the entire book of market makers and their bid and ask prices in addition to the amount of shares involved.

Level III (Level 3, L3, L III, Liii) – An advanced real-time quotation service only available to registered market makers to facilitate quoting and order execution.

Limit Order – An order condition to buy or sell a specific quantity of shares at a specific price over a specific period of time.

Liquidity – An indicator of a stock's price stability making trading that stock easier and less risky.

Long (Long Position) – Purchasing a stock with the intention that the stock value will rise. Also for purposes of taxes, long refers to the holding of a stock for a period longer than 12 months.

Long Term Capital Gains – The profit made off of the increase in the value of a stock over the purchase price held longer than one year.

Lot – The number of shares being bought or sold in a single transaction.

Margin – The practice of borrowing money, usually from your broker, to purchase stock in a special margin trading account.

Margin Call – A notification from your broker to deposit more money into your margin account to maintain the minimum requirements.

Market – A general term referring to the stock

market.

Market Capitalization (Market Cap) – The total market worth of all a company's outstanding stock.

Market Order – An order to buy or sell a stock as soon as possible at the best price at the time of order execution.

Market Maker (MM) – A firm referred to as a broker-dealer that holds a large position in a stock to ensure fluid trading of that stock.

Market Sector – A segment of the stock market relating to a specific industry.

Message Board (Board) – An electronic information platform where members interactively share information on defined topics.

Micro-Cap – A public company with an estimated market capitalization under $250 million.

Momentum (Momo) – The measure of a stock's price or volume, indicating movement in a particular direction.

Mutual Fund – A managed pool of investors' money used to purchase an assortment of securities.

Nano-Cap – A micro-cap company with capitalization below $50 million.

National Association of Securities Dealers Automated Quotations (Nasdaq) – An electronic stock exchange that facilitates the buying and selling of stocks often associated with the technology sector.

New York Stock Exchange (NYSE) – The largest stock exchange in the world hosting many of the world's biggest and best-known public companies.

Order Book – A Level 2 stock quote list of the buy and sell orders for a stock, including the number of shares being bought and sold as well as the market makers behind them.

Over-The-Counter (OTC) – An unlisted stock not traded on the major stock exchanges such as NYSE and can refer to a penny stock.

Paper Trade – The practice of using a stock-trading simulator to buy and sell stocks without the risk of using real money.

Parabolic – An upward move in a stock price, which forms a curve resembling a parabola on the stock's price chart.

Pattern Day Trader – A day trader defined by the

SEC that makes more than four day trades during a five business day period.

Penny Stock – A riskier micro-cap company with stock priced under $5.

Portfolio – All of the stocks you currently own in your brokerage account.

Position – A certain amount of shares owned of an individual stock.

Prospectus – An official document that gives information about a specific investment.

Qualitative Analysis – An analysis method evaluating a company's quantifiable data, such as products, customer reviews, and business information.

Quantitative Analysis – An analysis method evaluating a company based on financial data.

Quote – The most current stock price where a set amount of shares was traded.

Retail Investor – The average independent investor not associated with an investment firm or brokerage.

Securities and Exchange Commission (SEC) – The government agency that regulates stock markets in the United States protecting investors.

Security – A financial instrument representing ownership in a public company.

Sentiment – The general attitude of investors about a stock or market.

Share – A single unit of ownership of a publicly traded company.

Short-Term Capital Gains – The profit made off the increase in the value of a stock over its purchase price held less than one year.

Securities Investor Protection Corporation (SIPC) – A corporation sanctioned by the Securities Investor Protection Act of 1970 to insure the value of investor's brokerage accounts.

Slippage – The condition when the anticipated price of the stock at the time of order entry differs from the actual price at the time it is filled.

Speculate – The act of buying risky stocks in hopes of a large financial gain.

Spread – The difference between the bid and ask prices of a stock.

Stock – A security that represents ownership in a publicly traded company.

Stock Certificate – A physical certificate that represents a quantity of shares of ownership in a company.

Stockbroker (Broker, Representative) – A licensed person that executes stock orders to buy and sell on behalf of an investor usually for a fee.

Stop Order – A stock sell order with a set stop price entered in advance indicating when to execute the order.

Symbol (Ticker, Ticker Symbol) – A group of characters often letters that replace the full name of the stock in the exchange quoting system. An example would be AAPL for Apple Inc.

Time-in-Force (TIF) – An order condition specifying the duration an order is open before it is filled or expires.

Trade – The act of buying or selling a stock or the completion of an order to buy or sell a stock.

Trader – An individual investor who buys and sells stocks.

Transfer Agent – A financial entity that a public

company uses to manage accounts, issue shares, and maintain accounts for investors.

Volatility – A measure of uncertainty of a stock's price indicating a higher risk level.

Volume – The number of shares traded in a stock or market in a given period of time.

Wire Fund Transfer (Wire Transfer) – A transfer of money electronically through an international network of banking institutions from one account to another.

About The Author

Chad Austin has a B.A. from the University of
Southern Maine. He is a veteran quality assurance
professional with over 20 years' experience analyzing a
wide range of software and hardware products for
startups and Fortune 100 companies alike. In addition to
his business career, Austin is a stock trader, writer,
entrepreneur, motorcyclist, runner, health enthusiast,
scuba instructor, and former public educator. When not
working or writing, he can be found exploring the many
breathtaking roads, trails, and beaches in his home state
of California.

www.ingramcontent.com/pod-product-compliance
Lightning Source LLC
Chambersburg PA
CBHW070253190526
45169CB00001B/401